'"We're all on a journey." And this is a luminous journey of resilience, of faith, of joy and hope. What we all need now.'
BONNIE GREER OBE FRSL, PLAYWRIGHT AND NOVELIST

'Bishop Rose's autobiography captures the essence of a woman whose deep spirituality and unwavering commitment to justice have shaped the lives of countless individuals in both the UK and around the world. Her reflections on faith, leadership and resilience offer powerful lessons for readers from all walks of life … making this a must-read for anyone who seeks to challenge societal norms and live authentically.'
KANYA KING CBE, CEO OF MOBO

'Powerful, insightful and incredibly moving. *The Girl from Montego Bay* invites you into a world of remarkable resilience, sheer tenacity and deep familial love from strangers. Bishop Rose navigates a harsh childhood in her beloved tropical island to journey to another, where she faces a different set of challenges without the sunshine to compensate. Her one constant is her faith and indomitable self-belief.'
GILLIAN JOSEPH, NEWS ANCHOR AND JOURNALIST

'Bishop Rose Hudson-Wilkin is well known for her courage in speaking out for justice and for her commitment to those who suffer discrimination and prejudice. Her memoirs reveal exactly why she has been able to do this with such passion and integrity. Above all, the extraordinary stories of her childhood and early adulthood show her costly and lifelong obedience to Jesus Christ and her trust in a loving God, in spite of experiences that could have crushed her. Her story is unputdownable and unforgettable.'
THE REVD CHRISTINA REES CBE

'The powerful memoir of Bishop Rose Hudson-Wilkin ... a public theologian whose vision calls us all to live into the beloved community that God created us to be. This is not only a story of personal triumph, but also an Alleluia – an echo of faith, hope and love ... a gift that will inspire generations to come.'

THE VERY REVD SANDYE A. WILSON, INTERIM DEAN, CATHEDRAL OF ALL SAINTS, ST THOMAS, VIRGIN ISLANDS

'This is the most humane, humorous and enjoyable Episcopal autobiography in living memory. Rose's epic journey on the Montego Bay to Dover Express is packed with poignancy and passion with cameo appearances by The Queen, Speaker John Bercow, Bishop John Sentamu and husband Ken as the Bishop's rock. A must read.'

THE REVD JONATHAN AITKEN, AUTHOR AND BROADCASTER

THE GIRL FROM MONTEGO BAY

The Autobiography of Britain's
First Black Woman Bishop

Rose Hudson-Wilkin

First published in Great Britain in 2025

SPCK
SPCK Group
Studio 101
The Record Hall
16–16A Baldwin's Gardens
London EC1N 7RJ
www.spckpublishing.co.uk

Scripture quotations are taken from New Revised Standard Version Bible: Anglicised Edition, copyright © 1989, 1995 the Division of Christian Education of the National Council of the Churches of Christ in the United States of America. Used by permission. All rights reserved.

Scripture marked KJV is taken from the New King James Version. Copyright © 1982 by Thomas Nelson, Inc. Used by permission. All rights reserved.

Photographs courtesy of the author unless otherwise stated.

British Library Cataloguing-in-Publication Data
A catalogue record for this book is available from the British Library

ISBN 978-0-281-08960-4
eBook ISBN 978-0-281-08962-8

3 5 7 9 10 8 6 4

Typeset by Fakenham Prepress Solutions, Fakenham, Norfolk NR21 8NL
First printed in Great Britain by Clays

eBook by Fakenham Prepress Solutions, Fakenham, Norfolk NR21 8NL

Produced on paper from sustainable sources

Contents

List of plates	vii
Foreword	ix
Acknowledgements	xi
Introduction: My soul needs to sing!	1
1 Born in Montego Bay	7
2 The return of the mummy	21
3 Homecoming	33
4 Teach me	45
5 Stepping out	55
6 Back to Montego Bay	69
7 Till death do us part	77
8 It's cold!	91
9 Try, try and try again	99
10 Juggling motherhood and ministry	107
11 The journey to priesthood	119
12 Closing one door and opening another	129
13 Growing (both) families	137
14 Hackney, here I come!	149
15 Royal connections	163
16 Chaplain to the Speaker of the House of Commons	179
17 A call to be Bishop of Dover	207
18 Revelation	221

This book is dedicated to all the women and girls who have experienced and continue to experience abuse across the globe.

List of plates

1 Baby Rose in her mother's arms with Shirley and half-sister Beverley, late 1961
2 Father Joe, 1964
3 Shirley and Rose with Aunt Pet, 1964
4 Ken and Rose, engaged, Montego Bay, 1982
5 Ken and Rose on their wedding day with Ms Faye Jolly and Mr Horace Whittingham, Rose's adopted mom and daddy, 23 April 1983
6 Ken and Rose on their wedding day with parents Matthew and Audrey, Eunice and Joe, 1983
7 The day of Rose's priesting, 23 April 1994
8 Rose with sister Shirley at her first service after being ordained as priest, 1994
9 Rose enroute to a party, 1990
10 Rose with her famous placard in Dean's Yard after the vote in Synod in favour of women priests, 11 November 1992
11 Hannah, Jamie and Amanda on holiday, mid 1990s
12 'The vicar on the roof' and curate Richenda, All Saints Haggerston, 1999
13 Having a drink with Archbishop Desmond Tutu at the 2006 gathering of the World Council of Churches, Porto Alegre, Brazil
14 Skydiving to raise funds for All Saints Haggerston, 2007
15 Ken and Rose celebrating their twenty-fifth wedding anniversary, 2008

16 Hannah and David's wedding in Jamaica, 30 April 2011

17 Rose with her mother and grandson Arthur, 2015

18 President Barack Obama in Central Lobby, 25 May 2011, with Rose and Speaker John Bercow © House of Commons

19 Tributes paid to murdered Labour MP Jo Cox, Birstall, 17 June 2016. From left to right: Hilary Benn MP, Speaker John Bercow, Prime Minister David Cameron, Rose, Labour leader Jeremy Corbyn © Matt Cardy/gettyimages

20 Rose consecrated as Bishop of Dover at St Paul's Cathedral, London, 19 November 2019. From her left are the Bishop of Jamaica, the Archbishop of South Africa, the former Archbishop of York, John Sentamu, the Bishop of London, Sarah Mullally and the Archbishop of Canterbury, Justin Welby

21 Newly consecrated outside St Paul's Cathedral with singer Jermain Jackman, previous winner of BBC's *The Voice*

22 Rose's official invitation to the Coronation of King Charles III and Queen Camilla

23 The Queen Consort visits STORM Family Centre, London, 9 February 2023. Beside Rose are Kanya King MBE, founder of the MOBO Awards and Marie Hanson, CEO of S.T.O.R.M. © WPA Pool/gettyimages

24 King Charles and Rose in conversation at an exhibition of globes created for The World Reimagined (of which Rose is Patron) in Leeds Town Hall, November 2022

Foreword

The late South African president Nelson Mandela once famously declared, 'It always seems impossible until it is done.' His words could easily have been applied to the life of Rose Hudson-Wilkin, once a struggling, abandoned Jamaican child who would eventually become Chaplain to the Speaker of the House of Commons, recipient of the Queen's Honors and Britain's first Black Woman Bishop. Indeed, Rose exemplifies what Mandela described when he said, 'Everyone can rise above their circumstances and achieve success if they are dedicated to and passionate about what they do.'

It was dedication and passion – combined with the loving support from unexpected sources – that enabled Rose to press on as a child when her mother left her and her father neglected her, when life's options seemed bleak and any kind of abundant life appeared impossible. And it was dedication and passion – combined with a powerful awareness of God's presence and grace – that enabled Rose to press on in her sense of calling, precisely when the Church of her time and place said that a woman could work and work on behalf of the Church but not be allowed to become a priest. Through it all, Rose pressed on! 'Lord, I will be faithful to your calling,' she declared early on, 'and when the Church says yes to women, I will be ready.'

One cannot read Rose's story without thinking of the great women of Scripture who said yes to God's call on their lives.

Like Miriam the prophetess leading the people of God in song, and Deborah the judge leading them in battle. Like Mary of Nazareth daring to trust God even when others would see only scandal, and Mary of Magdala daring to believe even when the Jesus' closest friends refused to do so. Like Phoebe and Lydia and Junia and Priscilla and Tryphena and Tryphosa and Persis and Julia and all those faithful women who rolled up their sleeves and worked alongside the apostle Paul. The echoes of their stories, and those of other women in the Jesus Movement throughout the centuries, can be heard as you read Rose's story.

And one cannot read her story without … smiling. From the opening story of her encounter with her other great hero, Archbishop Desmond Tutu, to the delightful tale of staying over in the royal residence at the invitation of Queen Elizabeth and Prince Philip, there is a genuine exuberance in her narration that is both contagious and inspiring. With each turning of the page, one finds in Rose not just an impressive leader (which she most certainly is!), but also a fellow pilgrim and a companion in the Way of Love to which we all are called by the God who the Bible says, 'is love.'

The Most Rev. Michael B. Curry
XXVII Presiding Bishop of The Episcopal Church and author of *Love is the Way* and *Songs My Grandma Sang*

Acknowledgements

This book would not exist without the numerous women and men, young and old, who have regularly asked me over many years, especially after doing speaking engagements, if I have ever given thought to writing my story.

With their encouragement and that of my husband who relentlessly said to me, 'Rose, you can do it!', this book became possible.

I am thankful to Madeleine White who came alongside me at a time when I was beginning to feel like I was stuck and especially to my editor, Alison Barr who gave me much affirmation after reading every chapter, hence making me feel that I was on the right track.

I am tremendously lucky and thankful to have been called to serve the people in Hackney (the parish of Holy Trinity with St Philip, Dalston & All Saints, Haggerston) who loved me and made me feel that I was good enough when some of the challenging experiences I was having tried to say otherwise. I am thankful for Archbishop Sentamu, area Bishop of Stepney at the time, for his discerning spirit in agreeing to appoint me to that role. I describe my time with the people in Hackney, as the best years of my life!

But there was more to come. The wisdom of our late Queen Elizabeth II in inviting me to become one of her Chaplains made so much more possible. Thank you, John Bercow, for your confidence in appointing me to serve as the first female Chaplain to the Speaker of the House of Commons. And my thanks to the Archbishop of Canterbury and the people of the diocese of Canterbury for calling me to serve them as Bishop of Dover.

I owe a great depth of gratitude to some of the women and men in my life who never cease to pray for me: Margaret and Lawrie Patterson, Jo Kelly-Moore, Paulette Simpson, Margaret Sentamu, John Barton and all those in my present diocese who simply surround me with prayer. I must also thank Mary Beckles who's always willing to sort out my computer issues for me!

I am grateful to those who have loved and nurtured me in Montego Bay Jamaica: my Sunday School teachers, my god-mother (Viola Morle), Aunt Pet, Horace Whittingham and Faye Jolly, my big sister Shirley, who I still look up to and to all my friends across the globe (who are really like family) and who continue to journey with me.

I am indebted to my administrative staff team – Richard Braddy, Helen Hardwick, Fiona Medeiros and Tommy Geddes – whose efficient working has enabled me the space to carve out time to work on this book.

And finally, I am truly blessed to have the love and unwavering support of my beloved husband, Ken my three wonderful children, Amanda, Hannah and Jamie and my amazing grandchildren Jayden, Reece, Arthur, Gabriel, Cleopatra and Cosette.

INTRODUCTION
MY SOUL NEEDS TO SING!

A BALMY EVENING IN PORTO ALEGRE, Brazil. I was sitting at a hotel table with fellow Church of England delegates at the 2006 gathering of the World Council of Churches (WCC). Though deeply engrossed in conversation, we couldn't help but notice a distinctive figure in the foyer ... It appeared to be none other than the Archbishop of Cape Town. I could hardly contain my excitement.

'Let's invite him over,' I said. And without waiting for agreement, I jumped up and called, 'Excuse me!'

The figure turned around, and I finally found myself in the same space as my hero – renowned bishop, worldwide leader in the Anglican Communion and international figure for peace and reconciliation: Desmond Tutu. When he smiled, I felt myself enveloped by warmth; the fact that he was a giant on the world stage simply ceased to matter.

'Archbishop Tutu, would you consider joining us for a drink? We're over there.' I waved at my group bunched around a corner table. 'We'd love it if you would.'

Luckily, he said yes. What a moment! Before I knew it, he was sitting next to me, tasting my pina colada and regaling us with tales that kept us all chuckling for much of the evening. His faith and his joy were palpable. Little did I know that thirteen years later I'd be living in the house in Canterbury where he shared a kitchen supper with the former Bishop of Dover, Richard Third.

The news of Archbishop Tutu's passing, at the great age of ninety, came on Boxing Day 2021, just as I was beginning to pen my thoughts for this autobiography. My mind went back to the early nineties. I'd been invited to preach at evensong at Bath Abbey, and it was a surprise when the congregation erupted in applause at the end. The incumbent told me later, 'We've never before had people clapping during a service.' I believed him. This was no ordinary parish church going 'off piste'; this had to be of the Spirit! As we bid farewell to people at the door, one beautifully attired woman said to me, 'You must have some great ambition!'

'Yes,' I said rather eagerly. 'To meet Desmond Tutu and Nelson Mandela!'

What was it about these two giants that so attracted me? It had to be their ability to dance and laugh after all that they had endured. I loved their resilience, their hope, their way of living out the Christian faith, their uncompromising stance on justice. Most of all, I loved that they looked just like me! Their leadership and visible faith were deeply inspiring.

Indeed, my ambition was not only to meet them but to be like them. I too wanted to speak out uncompromisingly on behalf of the most vulnerable. I wanted to love, forgive, show compassion and exude the joy of the Lord, day by day, just as they did. I wanted to sing and dance, in and out of the Spirit, even if no one else was listening or watching. I wanted to live out my faith visibly. I had seen the struggle, pain and hardship of both their lives, and the fact that their childhoods had been tough, like mine, encouraged me further. I was determined that, going forward, my life wouldn't be shaped negatively by the challenging experiences I'd endured. I too was no one's victim! One of my 'go-to' pieces of Scripture is from Paul's second letter to the church in Corinth: 'We are afflicted in every way, but not crushed; perplexed, but not driven to despair; persecuted, but not forsaken; struck down, but not destroyed' (2 Corinthians 4:8–9, NRSV).

The fight for freedom and justice by Nelson Mandela and Desmond Tutu was not a private endeavour by two individuals for their personal benefit; it was to benefit a whole people. So much was done to dehumanise black South Africans (that is, all non-whites): they were segregated, beaten, crushed and treated as having very little or no value. Yet my heroes refused to believe the lie that they were of no worth. Archbishop Tutu's faith told him a different story from that which the Dutch Reformed Church had then shamefully preached and practised. His faith assured him that he was created in God's image; that he was loved with an everlasting love; that God sent his Son, Jesus Christ, to die for him; that God wanted him to have abundant life. There was nothing very abundant about the kind of lives people were expected to live in the townships, with their lack of amenities. Tutu and Mandela committed themselves to working for change – one by every peaceful means; the other 'by violent means if necessary'.

I understood their pain and rage. Even as a teenager, I'd shared their anger at the various atrocities perpetrated at each massacre in South Africa. I became aware, however, that much more was happening away from the cameras that was not being reported by the world's media. Sadly, I must confess I still feel rage welling up inside me every time I see or hear of the numerous injustices that continue to be committed around the world on different continents and in different contexts, such as the reported atrocities in Sudan and Yemen and towards the Rohingya Muslims in Myanmar and the Uyghurs in China. We have seen collective rage building too, exploding on our streets in the form of Black Lives Matter, and protests over Putin's war on Ukraine, Hamas's barbaric attack on Israel, and Israel's leaders' response of collective punishment in indiscriminately bombing Gaza, killing thousands of children, women and other non-combatants, and withholding water, medicine and food from the Palestinians.

As in Bath Abbey in the early nineties, today I am still praying and hoping for change; waiting, in the words of the prophet Amos, to see 'justice roll down like waters, and righteousness like an ever-flowing stream' (Amos 5:24).

I've already shared the story of my evening with Archbishop Tutu in Porto Alegre. In fact, the Appointments Committee of the General Synod had also invited me to be part of the delegation at the previous World Council of Churches, gathering in Harare, Zimbabwe, in 1998. I am so grateful to them, as it was there that I met President Nelson Mandela! He had been invited to address the WCC Assembly, and I made sure to position myself at the end of a row so that I could be in the right place, if allowed, for a sort of 'If I could just touch the hem of his garment' moment. Sure enough, as the President passed down the aisle, I extended my hand to him and he shook it. For a brief moment I was able to look into his eyes. An ambition fulfilled. My soul a-singing!

1
BORN IN MONTEGO BAY

WHEN I MADE MY ENTRANCE into the world at the beginning of 1961, Jamaica was still a British colony ruled from Westminster. It would be another eighteen months before the country finally won its independence. Almost 130 years earlier, slavery had been abolished but, in the words of the poet Langston Hughes, life was 'no crystal stair' for those born subsequently. Former slave masters may not have had the right in law to whip and order the once-enslaved population around, but in many ways they were still in charge.

It was as well that my grandmother, Francis Rebecca Matilda Ferguson (fondly known to everyone as Ms Fan), was a strong woman. With ten children to look after, she found employment breaking stones at the Frome sugar estate, and I can just imagine the labour force singing the old folk song as they worked, moving in line with its rhythm:

Guh dung a Manuel Road gal an bwoy fi go bruk rockstone.
Bruck dem one by one, gal an bwoy, finga mash no cry,
gal an bwoy, memba a play we a play, gal an bwoy ...

Although I only really saw my grandmother during a handful of summers as a teenager, I feel something of her resilience, her inner strength, flowing through my veins.

My mother, Eunice, gave birth to her first child when she was seventeen years old. I assume she had thought herself to be in love with the father, Hardy Christie, a local boy of similar age, though no mention was ever made of him. Ms Fan and my mother's four sisters (Mavis, Eulah, Carmen and Narissa) would have supported her during her pregnancy and labour, and the child, named Beverley, seems to have been embraced by the family. At some point, Eunice moved from the country and settled in Montego Bay with Beverley and my father, Joseph. Here, the local midwife discovered that my mother's second baby was in a breech position and arranged for her to be attended to at the local hospital. I have no idea if Eunice had sight of the Caribbean Sea from her bed, or whether she could hear the waves lapping along the hospital's walls (it has long since been relocated further inland). But I like to think the sights and sounds soothed her amid the fear of the delivery going wrong and the unrelenting pain of the contractions. She probably longed to have Ms Fan and my aunts nearer at this critical time. Happily, Shirley arrived safely, and three days after Eunice's twenty-fourth birthday, I did too!

I am not aware of the quality of the relationship my mother shared with our father, Joseph Hudson. He and his siblings (Ivan, Petrona, Louise and Estella) had been brought to Jamaica from Cuba by their mother, Salvina, when they were children. Aunt Pet (Petrona) told me that their father was a ship's captain, but we know nothing else of him. It's possible that Salvina was running from Castro's Cuba; sadly, what she found in Jamaica was equally uncompromising – so much so that it resulted in her having a major mental breakdown. She was committed to the country's main asylum, Bellevue

Hospital, in the capital, Kingston, at the other end of the island.

The family were never to see her again. Mental ill health had always carried a stigma, and Salvina would have been seen and referred to as a 'mad woman'. Years later, I discovered she had died while still a patient, and on receiving her death certificate I wept for the grandmother I had never known, whose dreams of a new life had become a nightmare, not only for her but for her five children. They must have been affected detrimentally, as in effect my father and his siblings brought themselves up. They were educated in the university of life as they eked out a living doing a little bit of this and a little bit of that.

All married eventually, except my father. I learned from my mother many years later that she once overheard Aunt Pet asking Joseph when he was going to propose. When he laughed out loud at the very thought, it could have been due to nervousness, to feeling unworthy of taking such a big step, but the result had huge repercussions for Shirley and me. Realising they had no future together, my mother departed for England a few months after my second birthday.

In fact, it was normal practice for one parent to migrate, then once working to save enough money to send for the other parent. Later, they would be in a position to bring over the children too. However, given the instability of my father and mother's relationship, this was destined never to happen. As it was, Aunt Pet had to quickly step in. She told me: 'Yuh modher lef oonnoo with oonnoo fadher, the man caan even luk afta imself, a pickney im a go luk afta.' (Your mother left you both with your father, but he cannot even look after himself. How is he going to look after children?)

With Aunt Pet assuming the responsibility of being our main carer, my father was off the hook. We moved into the home in River Bay Road that she shared with her husband Charlie, their daughter Juney and another niece, Gloria (whose mother had died). In fact, Joe had at least another couple of children by separate liaisons, but the reality was that he never knew how to be a father. He'd scarcely had a father figure himself, and his mother's influence, due to her mental illness, was short-lived. Fatherhood and being a husband were simply not in his DNA.

So Joe happily embraced a carefree lifestyle, showing up whenever he felt like it. He knew he would have to prepare himself for a good tongue-lashing from his big sister, but this he gladly endured, knowing that at some point she would calm down and offer him a hot meal. I do have a precious memory of him allowing me a few sips of his bottle of Guinness in a rare demonstration of affection.

Guinness was one of the ingredients of a special drink the adults would concoct most Sundays. They called it a tonic, and it did contain some healthy things, such as grated carrots, beetroot, nutmeg and beaten raw eggs, along with condensed milk, but it certainly packed a punch, due to the alcohol content, and as children we were only given a small quantity. Nowadays, I just go for the shorthand version: add the condensed milk to a bottle of Guinness, relax and enjoy a taste from the past!

Aunt Pet's family were no more tactile than my father – there were no kisses or hugs; no 'well done's. Though Shirley and I were very small, six and five years old respectively, when we began accompanying Aunt Pet to the market in downtown Montego Bay every Saturday morning, she never offered to hold our hands. Rather, we were instructed to hold on to her dress or the baskets she was carrying. We did not allow ourselves to be distracted by children playing near the wooden shacks in the yards we passed, surrounded by a mix of barbed wire and zinc fencing. We knew that we couldn't afford to be distracted by anything, including those selling sweets or savoury items, because finding her again would be a near-impossible task. It would have been heavy work for Aunt Pet, walking around with the shopping. So, as young as we were, we were expected to be useful and carry a small package for the journey home, the weight of which increased as we got older!

Our formal education began in the kindergarten school organised by the Seventh-day Adventist Church. Shirley and I learned nursery rhymes – 'Baa Baa Black Sheep', 'London's Burning', 'London Bridge is Falling Down' and 'Ten Green Bottles', to name but a few. I remember those years as largely carefree ones, full of fun, though even as tiny children we knew that those who taught us must be obeyed. Teachers carried as much authority as our parents did and could discipline with the strap if we stepped out of line. In the playground during break time, however, we were allowed to explore and play to our hearts' content. There was nothing like a risk assessment policy in place; we simply had to be sensible and learn from every fall which stone or patch of ground to avoid. The scars on my knees today bear witness to some of those early self-taught lessons.

Not long after I began kindergarten, the Anglican episcopal church of St James – the main parish church in Montego Bay, where I had been baptised at three months old – planted a mission church, St Francis. The mission saw the need for another prep school, and it was decided Shirley and I would start going there.

The school was up a short, steep hill; as a small child it felt to me as if I were climbing a mountain! There were no pavements, so Shirley and I had to navigate the traffic by always being alert and looking in all directions. It was not long before we began to use a shortcut, which was also rather dangerous as we had to cross a busy road with impatient taxi drivers going at speed, and in addition we had sharp jagged rocks to negotiate. Looking back now and remembering the terrain as a parent and grandparent, I feel horrified.

Back at home, in contrast to the freewheeling lifestyle of our occasionally present father, there was, as I've suggested, structure and boundary. Shirley and I were apportioned tasks according to our age. The wooden floor of the house had to be dyed with a red dye, and although the adults and our older cousins undertook this heavy work, we were not considered too young to learn how to do the shining once the dye had dried. Given a brush made from old coconuts that were no longer edible, cut in half and dried out in the sun, we were told to keep going until the adults could see their faces reflected!

Another chore we were tasked with, when we moved to Glendevon in 1965, was to fill the large oil drum pan with water. In the UK, oil drum pans are mainly used to make calypso music at large festivals such as the Notting Hill Carnival, or as containers for cooking the jerk chicken or pork over a barbecue.

In Jamaica in the 1960s, however, running water was rarely piped directly into people's homes, unless they had the means to rent or purchase somewhere a bit more expensive.

(The new social houses provided by the government did have running water and an indoor toilet.) Otherwise, the oil drum pan was placed where it would easily catch rainwater from specially placed zinc directed from the roof towards it. When no rain fell, it was the job of the children to keep the drum pan filled up with water from the stand-pipe, which could be a short or a long distance away. Luckily for Shirley and me, ours was nearby. How many hundreds of journeys we made over the years to fill up that drum pan! It was a delight when there was a heavy downpour to do the job for us.

Aunt Pet and our father continued to have a kind of love/hate relationship. We would listen to their disagreements from a distance, as we were not allowed to be in the same space when they were having 'big people's conversation'. If perchance we were standing too close, we were shouted at: 'Go whey and stop tek the wud outa mi mout' (Go away and stop taking the words from my mouth).

Aunt Pet did offer Joe encouragement, however, even if he did not recognise it as such. I'm sure she was behind him being able to purchase a two-roomed house on the new government housing scheme, two and a half miles outside Montego Bay, in Rosemount, in 1964. When the six of us moved in with him, this living arrangement lasted less than a year. My father and Aunt Pet were constantly arguing, and that spurred her and the rest of the family to move out and rent a property in Glendevon. There, Shirley and I began attending Albion All Age School. It was about a mile and a half away and for the first few days an adult would accompany us there and back. However, as there were lots of children making the same journey, we were soon allowed to go with them. Again, of course, there were no pedestrian crossings with friendly lollipop men or ladies. We simply had to keep alert. We had all been warned by our guardians of the dangers of playing on the road and knew we could be scolded by any adult along the route to and from school.

It has probably become clear by now that caring adults were not always much of a reality in my life. Indeed, sometimes, under the guise of care, they got things very wrong. I can't recall quite what age I was when a dispute arose between another primary school pupil, Loveta Fletcher, and me. It was short-lived, because after the exchange of a few punches I realised that she had a big weight advantage! I retreated, much to the disappointment of the gathered crowd of children who were walking with us. As their 'excitement' had been cut short, they tried to encourage phase two. By then, having come to my senses and remembered that fighting was not something I should be doing, I crossed over the road.

Unfortunately, Aunt Pet's sister Louise had decided to come and meet me and, finding me in the wrong place, demanded an explanation. The children were quick to volunteer that I'd been involved in a fight; that it had been Loveta who'd started it and she'd had the last hit. Aunt Lou was quieter than Aunt Pet, but if I was hoping to be commended for walking away from conflict, I was in for a shock. My aunt felt that I'd been hard done by and decided to take up my case. She told me that I should hit the girl. 'Lick her!' she shouted at me. 'Lick her!' I was confused and shocked that an adult was encouraging a fight. Something inside me said this was wrong, so I refused to respond to her urging, and stood still. This angered my aunt. I was publicly disobeying her. Before I knew it, she had reached for a branch from a nearby tree and I was being whipped for not following her instructions. So not only had I been hit by a classmate, but now I had to take a beating for being a peacemaker. I was left utterly confused and embarrassed by her 'assault' on me.

Though Shirley and I had been taught road safety, there were other dangers to navigate: men and older boys could be more of a risk to us young girls than being hit by a car. We had to stay alert, because what might at first appear to be an innocent offering of a fruit in season could prove to have nasty strings attached. By word of mouth, we learned who to avoid and the places where we needed to make sure we stayed in larger groups. From childhood into my teenage years, and even in adulthood, men and boys on street corners were inclined to call out to us, to smile at us or to make suggestive moves with their hands – and sometimes with other parts of their bodies! When we lived in Glendevon, our bathroom was an outdoor zinc construction a short distance from the house. As I grew up, I would carefully check that no one was around and sometimes take another family member to keep watch. Looking back now, I recall that this sense of feeling threatened, though very real, was unspoken, and I cannot help but wonder if this contributed to the abuse I suffered never being mentioned. However, at a recent speaking engagement, as memories resurfaced, I felt able to name it openly. More will be said later in this story.

Although I'd been baptised in the parish church of St James, it was at the newly built St Francis Mission Church that the rhythm of Anglicanism gradually became part of my own heartbeat. The Church in Jamaica back then was very much in 'pioneer' mode. Although we did not have a full complement of priests or many resources, that did not prevent those who were in ministry roles from being ambitious. With a passion for the gospel that swept everyone forward, men and women from the main parish churches would prayerfully take the lead and start fledgling worshipping communities in other neighbouring communities. This, of course, was how St Francis had come about.

Our elderly lay reader, Mr Corbett, was very wise. On the Sundays when there was no priest, he and the Church Army officer, Captain Daniels, would encourage us children to read the lessons, take up the collection and lead the choruses and, eventually, the prayers of intercession. Every fifth week was special – it was Youth Sunday. And every year, our excellent Sunday school teachers would help us put on an Easter play and a Christmas production, which were well supported by the local community.

To my delight, a mobile library used to come regularly to St Francis. At a very early age I had discovered a real love for reading, and it was thrilling to be able to choose the two books we were allowed. Growing up in a very poor environment, reading gave me a window into how others in the world lived; it opened possibilities that I never would otherwise have imagined.

The one book that had a prominent place in our home – and in Aunt Lou's – was the Bible. If Aunt Lou heard my sister and me playing too loudly outdoors, she would call us, 'Marine an Rose, you mekking too much noise out dere. Come in an read di Bible.' We did not hesitate to obey. It was the Psalms that we were mostly directed to read – not a pleasurable experience for a young child who would rather be playing hide and seek or climbing a tree. And there were plenty of trees to climb on the vacant lot next to where we lived. Yet reading for Aunt Lou (even if under duress) and at church gave me a biblical literacy that I would in later years come to appreciate. Little did I know the foundation that was being laid.

Aunt Lou liked us to sleep over with her if her husband, Ralph Hunter, was away in the country. Indeed, on one occasion when I was staying, a burglar broke in, and by the time I'd woken up and realised what was happening, he was asking for a match. I foolishly said I knew where the matches were kept, while my aunt elbowed me in the ribs as if to say, 'Keep quiet, girl!' However, having lit the lamp, looked around and realised there was nothing of value to steal, the burglar climbed back through the window after being given something to eat and the few dollars that my aunt swore were all she had. Very early the next morning, Aunt Lou saw me back to Aunt Pet's and, without any explanation, went to report the incident at the police station in town. It was never spoken about within the family again.

Something else I learned from listening in on conversations was that Aunt Lou's penchant for garlic had nothing to do with its taste (she was a great cook) and everything to do with believing it to ward off ghosts. It would be fair to say that this dear soul had her demons. Life had dealt her and her siblings a heavy blow. Although she had two adult children, we rarely saw them, and their father was never in the picture or spoken about.

Someone who had long been absent from my own life, however, was about to make a momentous return.

2
THE RETURN OF
THE MUMMY

UNTIL I WAS EIGHT OR NINE, all the talk was that my mother had gone to England and forgotten about us. Shirley and I did not really believe this, as the occasional package would arrive. One contained two dolls, and these lasted the duration of our childhood in Montego Bay, though towards the end an arm was missing here and a leg there! My mother also sent us each a watch, but Aunt Pet, fearing we would not look after these properly, never allowed us to wear them.

We grew very used to Aunt Pet making disparaging remarks about both our parents in our hearing – how neither of them was contributing to our well-being; how grateful we should be to her for looking after us. I can see now that she did have a compassionate heart, but the burden of caring for other people's children (even if they were family) had made her feel taken for granted. And it was a great disappointment that my mother had not followed the usual custom of those living abroad and sent home (in addition to the occasional presents for Shirley and me) barrels of food items and clothing for Aunt Pet and everyone else. On a good day, this was not mentioned; however, on a bad day, we would not hear the end of it.

After she moved to England, Eunice met and married Vincent Bernard, who hailed from St Elizabeth, Jamaica, and they had started a brand new family. We later learned that they were planning to return and were looking to purchase a house, and even at eight years old I found myself looking at every property with a 'For Sale' sign outside – dreaming of one with many more bedrooms than the two the nine of us (Gloria and Juney had three children between them) were currently sharing. Shirley and I hoped that things were going to get very much better.

The great day of arrival came. It was difficult to focus on classwork that morning, such was the mix of excitement and trepidation we were feeling at the prospect of seeing our mother for what seemed like the first time. I had no memory at all of what she looked like – after all, I was still only a baby when she left. We rushed home from school, and there she was – taking it easy in the rocking chair.

'Go ahead, speak to you madder,' I heard my aunt say.

But I was speechless. In my head, I could hear myself repeating, 'She is pretty and she is my mother.' Yet she was also a stranger. I seemed incapable of feeling anything but curiosity. I have no memory of what was discussed that afternoon, what time she left or how the day ended. However, it transpired that plans were being made for Shirley and me to go and live with my mother and step-father and their four children – Angela, Janet, Briant (Chris) and Clive (Garth would be a later addition to the family) – at a home they had bought in Kingston, the capital of Jamaica.

So it was that in February 1970, when Shirley was ten years old and I had just turned nine, Eunice was suddenly back in our lives. Determined to return to Kingston with us the very next day, she demanded we gather up our meagre belongings in haste and gave us no time to say goodbye to our friends at school and church. I'm not sure if we cried as we waved farewell to the only family we had ever known, or indeed if there were any tears from either of my aunts. My memory is that it was all very matter-of-fact.

The three of us headed to the station in downtown Montego Bay, not far from River Bay Road, where my mother had given birth to me. I do recall that there was no rush for the train, as the driver seemed quite content to wait for everyone to get on board before slowly pulling out. This being our first trip to Kingston, Shirley and I were keen to absorb all we saw. At every stop, people were selling their wares – sweets, fruits and vegetables, nuts and snow cones (shaved ice in a paper cone with syrup added to it) – normally a great favourite with us children. Some traders would actually board the train to try to encourage more passengers to buy their goods. There were preachers too, inviting people to repent from their wicked ways! So much noise and activity helped to distract us from the fact that we were on our way to live with total strangers, who were, in fact, family.

Everyone was there when we arrived at 5 Moore Street: Vincent Bernard, a very tall, good-looking man, and four-year-old Angela, three-year-old Janet, one-year-old Chris and baby Clive. There were two houses on the premises. One was rented to multiple tenants, who occupied different rooms but shared kitchen and bathroom facilities. The house that the family lived in, though larger than the one we'd left in Montego Bay, actually had no more bedrooms. My mother and Mr Bernard occupied the master bedroom (with the baby in a cot), and the rest of us shared the second, which had a double bed and two singles.

It became clear very early on that, being older, we were to assume a good deal of responsibility. I remember the children asking for 'cuppa tea' regularly (the teabags were stored in a large black sack). So much tea was drunk, in fact, that my own days of tea drinking became numbered! Shirley and I were also to look after our young siblings and tidy up after them, especially when rice was on the menu (it always needed scraping up off the floor). There was no rest from the endless tasks of providing care and doing housework, but at least we were spared filling an oil drum pan, as the stand-pipe was in the middle of the yard and easily accessible from the living quarters.

One Saturday morning, a letter arrived for me. It was from my godmother in Montego Bay, Viola Morle (known to all as Ms Maud). She had written, 'Please say How-dy-do to your mother for me,' but when I shared this greeting, my mother reached over very fast and slapped me, telling me not to be silly. She was working at the sink at the time, and her wet hand stung my face.

'The word is "hello",' she snapped. 'Learn to pronounce the word right.'

Inside I was screaming, 'But that's exactly what the letter said!' I knew it would be disastrous to answer back. Yet why would my mother be upset that I was speaking to her in patois instead of proper English? I was beginning to feel she was impossible to please or understand. There was never a loving arm around us, showing us how to do a particular task, or a patient explanation of what was required. We were expected simply to know by virtue of our age!

We would be despatched on errands to the shop, never with a list, yet sure of a beating if we failed to bring back the correct items. There was an occasion when I was sent for either vanilla or soy sauce, but by the time I arrived at the shop, I had forgotten which one. I was fearful the whole journey home and did get into trouble for guessing wrongly. (To this day, I still cannot remember what I was meant to be buying!) As well as failing to show tenderness, Eunice seemed to have no understanding that we might be missing our friends and family back in Montego Bay. Everything felt harsh.

We'd begun attending Whitfield Primary School. My form teacher was the kindly Mrs Gravesandy, and Shirley's teacher, Mrs Johnson, was a fine woman too. One afternoon, we were informed that there would be a school trip to the Water Commission the next day. The cost was 15 cents per child, and we were asked to bring the money with us. When I told my mother, she did not acknowledge she had heard what I said, and I did not dare repeat myself. The next morning at school, as the register was being called, we were asked to give our 15 cents to the teacher. I sheepishly went up and explained that I had told my mother about the trip, but she hadn't given me any money. As I was a good student, Mrs Gravesandy offered to pay my fare herself.

We duly boarded the coach and set off, but I was beset by anxiety. Would the trip end promptly enough for us to be back at school at the time we usually left? It was my responsibility to collect my younger sisters, Angela and Janet, from the nursery nearby.

My worst fears were realised. The bus was an hour late, and I guess Shirley ended up collecting the children. As I set out for home on yet another fear-filled walk, I felt as if I was carrying the weight of the world on my shoulders.

Predictably, my mother refused to listen to why I'd been delayed and immediately struck me not just once, but with multiple blows. She then reached for a piece of board nearby and continued hitting me with that. My step-father did nothing to stop her, but rather added fuel to the fire by saying that I should not have gone on the school trip, because 'the water company dem tief people money'. (Receiving the ever-increasing water bills that regularly arrived in the post meant many cried foul and felt cheated.)

At one stage, the piece of board caught me by my left eye and blood began trickling down my face. Yet my mother was unstoppable, relentless. Luckily, my step-father's two brothers, Uncle Lusan and Uncle Pappason, came on the scene just then and immediately intervened. However, even when they got between my mother and me, it took some time before one of them managed to restrain her and eventually calm her down. I was terrorised by the experience. It added considerably to the sense of fear I felt being in that home.

My mother showed no interest in seeing what damage had been done, and the next day I was despatched to school and told to say I had fallen and hit my eye. With my face swollen, the injury was bad enough for me to be sent to the nearby clinic to receive medical attention. I wondered at the time if the nurses or my teachers believed my story, but no one questioned me further. It's sad to say that Shirley and I almost got used to feeling continually on edge. We never knew when our mother would lash out at us. It could be for something as silly as not returning an object to its rightful place.

Another incident still haunts me. My cousin Nellie was visiting from the country during the school holidays. Eunice had cooked chicken that Saturday evening and Nellie decided to take a piece out of the pot – something my sister and I would never have done, even in our wildest dreams. Unfortunately for us, my mother must have counted the pieces of chicken and when she realised one was missing demanded, 'Who did it?' We all said that it was not us. We did not want to tell on Nellie. My mother proceeded to accuse me of stealing the chicken, but my sister and I still did not give Nellie up. Perhaps we were afraid Eunice would beat her as mercilessly as she did us.

Next morning, as I was having breakfast with my siblings, she suddenly came into the dining room, pulled me from the table, held me by the throat and picked up the large bread knife. I could feel the point of the blade on my neck.

'Tell me who tek di chicken, odderwise mi kill you,' she shouted.

Right there and then I believed she would do me mortal harm and at that point I heard myself yell, 'Is Nellie. Nellie tek the chicken!'

She let go of me and I fell to the floor in a heap, crying, terrified and believing in that moment that my mother was completely crazy. How else could I explain the behaviour she had just displayed? Although I was still young, I knew this was not the normal conduct of a parent towards a child. The words of the psalmist I had read to my aunt – 'In my distress I called upon the LORD; to my God I cried for help' (Psalm 18:6) – came back to me. They were no longer words in a book, written hundreds of years before, but an absolute lifeline. I truly needed assistance. I was crying out to my God, both with tears and without.

Only our step-uncles and later my mother's brothers, when they were visiting, would come to our rescue when we were being beaten. Perhaps they were part of the answer to my prayer. Nonetheless, Shirley and I decided to write a letter to Aunt Pet back in Montego Bay. In this we documented the hardships we were experiencing, how we were being treated and how items our aunt had recently sent had not been given to us but shared with the rest of the family. We poured our hearts out, and by the time we had finished, there was a mass of pages to try to stuff into the envelope. So naive were we that we provided sender details, carefully printing our names and address on the back. Posting that letter gave us a sense of relief. Now our folks back in Montego Bay would know what our lives were like here with our mother. Hopefully, they would be so horrified they would come and take us away.

Unknown to us, the letter was returned to our home address while we were at school. Maybe it was too bulky. Maybe we hadn't stuck enough stamps on. Whatever the case, we came home one afternoon to discover the wind blowing lots of bits of torn paper, inscribed with our handwriting, all over the yard. The letter clearly hadn't made it to our aunt. Even more clearly, it had been opened and read by our mother! Surely this would result in a beating. My sister and I were utterly on edge.

However, there was no immediate reaction. Could we possibly have touched a raw nerve? Had Eunice been alarmed to read about how we were feeling? We continued to live in fear, nonetheless. Grown-ups used to say that they did not eat rice when it was hot. In other words, long after you'd been lulled into believing they had forgotten something, they would resurrect it. There might yet be an eruption of volcanic proportions that, given my recent encounter with the bread knife, could prove deadly.

Recently, I attended a reading at Lambeth Palace library of a letter written by an enslaved but literate woman living in one of the Caribbean islands. She described to the then Archbishop of Canterbury the conditions of those who were being kept in bondage. We do not know if the letter was ever received by the intended recipient, but it is believed that it was found and that the woman was punished for the crime of daring to tell her story. As the reading unfolded, I found myself becoming tearful. Memories resurfaced and I was engulfed again by the fear I'd known as a child, along with empathy for that poor woman and all she must have endured.

It is difficult to say why our mother decided not to treat us in her usual manner for this 'misdemeanour'. Quite possibly she was incensed (or even hurt?) to read of my longing to go back to our old home, and this prompted her to devise a punishment so callous I still struggle to understand it today. With no consultation or the slightest acknowledgement of the huge emotional impact it would have, she decreed that Shirley and I – who had been through so much together – were to be separated.

And so, in the summer of 1971 – approximately seventeen months after we had arrived in Kingston – Shirley was retained to help look after the house and the children, and I was sent back, on my own, to live with my aunt in Montego Bay.

3
HOMECOMING

SLIPPING BACK INTO LIFE IN MONTEGO BAY was not too difficult in some ways. I returned to my old school and my old church, and managed to rekindle previous friendships with ease. At home, due to the sheer relief of escaping the brutality of my time in Kingston, things felt better at first. Before long, though, Aunt Pet was regularly reminding me that my mother did not want me, and that I should be grateful she had taken me back. This is not the kind of conversation a young child should ever be involved in.

Looking back, I do not believe that Aunt Pet meant me any deliberate psychological harm. Life was tough and the household barely had enough to cover the necessities, never mind stretch to an extra mouth to feed. It transpired that my mother had given no hint that my time in Kingston was not working out prior to sending me back to Montego Bay. It was simply taken for granted that Aunt Pet would pick up the pieces, and I was returned like an unwanted package in the post. My aunt received no financial recompense for the years she had spent caring for my sister and me; nor did my parents offer any spoken appreciation.

With little money available, Aunt Pet had to eke out a living from whatever her husband brought home. Mas Charlie worked for the Electricity Company, clearing the undergrowth from around the light poles during the week.

On weekends, when the weather was good, he'd go fishing with one or two men in a small dugout canoe. Early on Saturday mornings, I'd be commandeered to accompany Aunt Pet to the seaside with his breakfast. I did enjoy these outings, as there would be crabs, prawns and crayfish for us to take back home, prepare and feast on as a reward. But this free seafood certainly wasn't enough to meet the needs of all the family. I'd regularly hear my aunt say, 'In God mi trus' (In God I trust). That trust was rewarded, as we would never go to bed hungry. There was always food of some sort for us to eat: God did indeed provide.

Typical of so many men of his generation, Mas Charlie was a functioning alcoholic. He was very present but not engaged (unlike my father, who was rarely either). Usually, after an evening of heavy drinking, he would eventually find his way home in the dark, occasionally slipping and falling. If he had not returned by the time it was very late, Aunt Pet would send me out to scour the local establishments, and there he would be, propping up some rum bar. (I would only be allowed in to coax him to leave and come home.) You would know he was very drunk, because he would be singing with gusto. Intriguingly, he would naturally select songs that were deeply religious – the old hymns, such as 'What Can Wash Away My Sin? (Nothing but the Blood of Jesus)' or 'Amazing Grace'. These clearly offered him some solace, and he would often sing himself to sleep.

Mas Charlie's drink of choice was Wray & Nephew overproof white rum, and he always kept a few bottles at home. Once, when I was about six or seven years old and meant to be playing with Shirley outside, I slipped indoors and drank a few mouthfuls. This was powerful stuff! Suddenly,

I realised I could not walk in a straight line. Realising, even at that tender age, that this must be connected to the drink I'd had from the bottle, and not wanting anyone to find out, I approached my sister and said, 'Let's play stagger.' It was my hope that no one would notice I was, in effect, drunk. I won!

After the game, I curled up on the floor and fell asleep. Unfortunately, Mas Charlie did notice there was less rum in the bottle than when he'd last had a drink. Aunt Pet was indignant. 'Nobady here drink yuh rum. Yuh drink too much and dat's affecting yuh memory' (Nobody here in the house has had any of your rum. You're drinking too much and you've forgotten how much rum you had in the bottle).

I knew otherwise!

Shirley, of course, was never far from my thoughts. We wrote regularly, but censored ourselves, knowing full well that others might end up reading our letters. Years later, I discovered she had cried daily after I was sent back to Montego Bay, even sobbing herself to sleep. Sadly, if my mother caught her, she would shout, 'Mek mi give yuh someting to cry for,' and beat her. On my first visit to Shirley's home in California when we were adults, she literally wailed as we said goodbye, and for a long time the memory of our forced separation as children was relived each time we parted. Thankfully, my dear sister has now devised a way of handling things better. She drives me to the airport, helps me get my bags out of the car and then after a quick hug, and a mutual glance that says so much, quickly drives away.

But though desolation was no stranger to me, there were real compensations to be found back at St Francis Mission. The lay reader, Mr Corbett, was still there, as supportive as ever of us young people, and our youth fellowship flourished. Other committed adults who gave of their time included Ms Faye Jolly, a single parent of a young boy, who was kind and attentive, and always ready to say 'well done'. We formed a close bond and decided to adopt each other: she became my mom and I became her daughter. I was also close to my best friend Pauline's mother, Gemoline Gillette. When I was at their home she too became my mom. You can imagine how much these surrogates meant to me, given the tough home environment that was still my lived experience. Looking back, it's obvious I was seeking compensation for the love and care my own mother was unable to offer. Nonetheless, with these new adults in my life, the melancholy song 'I'm nobody's child', that so appealed to unhappy youngsters like me around that time ceased to whir around my head quite so frequently.

Even now, I have a real emotional bond with these two wonderful women who showered me with affection. I still call them Mommy and they both refer to me as their daughter.

Like everyone else my age, I took the eleven-plus examination. The result would determine the secondary school I attended, and it was a thrill to see my name listed in the national newspaper and discover I had won a place at the prestigious Montego Bay High School.

Church Army officer Captain Kerr and his wife Clarissa were a great source of strength, helping Aunt Pet to source second-hand Montego Bay High School uniforms (Jamaican schools are renowned for their immaculate uniforms and here the girls wore a grey tunic with a green and white striped shirt) and a few basic textbooks. Aunt Pet was determined that although we were poor, I'd be well turned out, because, after all, I would be representing the family. In fact, there were emotional nuances I was probably not old enough to understand. Aunt Pet's daughter Juney had also won a place at the school some years before, but an unplanned pregnancy had meant she'd had to leave without fulfilling her potential – a real disappointment to the family. Now Aunt Pet had a second chance with me, and I am truly grateful to her for the sacrifices she made to help me thrive. On numerous occasions, I'd hear her say, 'Go a school and get yuh education, cause once yuh ave yuh education, nobady can tek it weh from yuh.'

She and others like her truly believed that. But what Aunt Pet appeared not to understand was that in order to achieve success, I needed to be released from some of the never-ending chores in order to have time to do my homework!

Staying behind to study at school or in the library was not an option. It's possible Aunt Pet feared I might become distracted or, worse still, end up in the same condition as my cousin. Asking that I be home by a certain time may have been her way of protecting me.

There were other challenges too. In my first year, I would be given JA$1.50 per week, but as things got worse financially for the family, this was reduced to JA$1. Transport to school cost me 30 cents, so after one day I simply had to walk. As for food, it was not always possible to take in things from home as I'd done in primary school (though there I was mocked because my drinks were water mixed with sugar, and my bread or bulla cake had no filling, such as cheese or ham). Luckily, a few of my friends would share their lunch with me.

This uneven level of support took its toll. I started in the A stream, but found myself dropping back a grade each year. By the time I got to the fifth-form, I was placed in 5X, having found it almost impossible to achieve anything like my potential. The fact that I was trying was recognised, though, and when I was rewarded by being made a prefect, I wore my badge with much honour.

I was fourteen years old when I preached my first sermon! I'd grown used to leading and speaking at the familiar mission church, but this occasion was to be in the parish church of St James during a wider deanery service. Climbing up the stairs to the pulpit, I felt both excited and scared. My text was Psalm 8:4: 'What are human beings that you are mindful of them, mortals that you care for them?' (NRSV). In effect, the sermon was a conversation between me and God. Who was I that he cared enough to send his Son to die for me? With all I'd experienced in my childhood, the question had real resonance. The fact was that I had started to sense something changing in me. Deep down, I knew that God was at the centre of it; that God was beginning to make a difference in my life.

One night a few weeks later, I had a disturbing dream. In it I was on the veranda in the dark, when someone called to me from below: 'Can I come up and be with you?'

My dream-self responded in alarm, 'No! I can't invite you up – I don't know who you are!'

The voice got louder and more emphatic: 'Let me come up! I want to be with you.'

My dream-self was so perturbed I began groping for the light switch.

And then came a different voice: 'Do not let him in! He is of the devil.'

I immediately had an incredibly strong sense of the rightness, the goodness, of this second voice. Overcome, I began praising and thanking God for making himself known to me – so loudly, in fact, that I woke up not only myself, but the whole household.

Still seeking reassurance, I reached for my Bible. It fell open at Luke 4 and I read:

> The Spirit of the Lord is upon me, because he has anointed me to bring good news to the poor. He has sent me to proclaim release to the captives and recovery of sight to the blind, to let the oppressed go free, to proclaim the year of the Lord's favour.
> (Luke 4:18–19)

Soothed by this passage, I dropped straight back to sleep. The next morning, reaching as usual for my Bible study booklet, I found that the allocated reading for the day was from Isaiah 61. I noticed with astonishment that it was the passage Jesus was reading from when he opened the scroll handed to him in the synagogue – the exact same passage I had read in the middle of the night!

> The Spirit of the Lord God is upon me, because the Lord has anointed me; he has sent me to bring good news to the oppressed, to bind up the broken-hearted, to proclaim liberty to the captives, and release to the prisoners; to proclaim the year of the Lord's favour ...
> (Isaiah 61:1–2)

This was the point when I began to recognise the beginning of my call to ministry. As my awareness and openness grew, I was thrilled to find many other scriptures seemed to be encouraging me – such as when Jeremiah says he's only a child and cannot speak. I had been hurt and abused, I had felt lost and alone, but now I knew that God's hand was on my life and my pain would not be in vain. Somehow it would be used for his glory.

At that time in Jamaica, women were very much a part of the life of the church. They made things happen! They opened and closed the buildings, they cleaned, they prepared the altar. However, they were not allowed to preside at the service of Holy Communion or give the absolution.

I found myself asking my bishop: 'How is it, when you have told us how important the sacrament is, that so many churches are prevented from having Holy Communion because no male priest is available? Aren't there women we could ordain who might lead in these places?' I felt I could hardly tell him directly of my calling to priestly ministry, but his intent gaze and wry smile suggested he had an inkling of where I was going with the conversation.

'Rose, we are Anglicans. We don't do that.'

I smiled and thought, *You may not do it and the church may not do it, but I know that God does.* Deep down I felt that God might just have other plans, and after that talk I made a promise: 'Lord, I will be faithful to your calling, and when the church says yes to women, I will be ready.'

It never occurred to me to leave the Anglican Church to seek out another church that embraced women in leadership. The Anglican Church had always been my spiritual home and I really believed that God was calling me to serve there.

I was prepared to wait and be led by the Spirit.

4
TEACH ME

AS THE TIME TO TAKE MY O-LEVELS drew near, I had to face reality: Aunt Pet simply could not afford to fund my education any longer. The only option was to find work. Fortuitously, a friend of mine mentioned that her father, who was a headmaster in a rural school, was advertising for pre-trained (that is not yet qualified) teachers. I decided to seek God's guidance in prayer. Then, feeling led by the Spirit, I filled in an application form and sent it off, without a word to my aunt.

On the morning of one of my exams, the headmistress Ms Lindsay summoned me to her office and told me there was a telegram for me. However, she refused to hand it over until the end of the day. I got through the exam somehow, fretting about whether it was from Kingston (from my sister Shirley, or perhaps even my mother), and then hotfooted my way back to the office to find out. Ripping the envelope open, I discovered I was being invited to an interview.

It transpired that Maldon Secondary School needed a PE and RE teacher. And so, a week later, I found myself on a bus bound for a village I didn't know at all. Aunt Pet had voiced concern that I was going so far away from home, but for me there was nothing to worry about. Things felt right. The Church might not yet be ready for women, but God had made me 'beautifully and wonderfully' into the young woman I had become. This is a phrase I have repeated time and again in my life – there is even a picture of me in *The Guardian* holding a placard that reads: 'WOMEN beautifully and wonderfully made in the image of God!' Here and now, at just seventeen, I knew God would find a way. I believe it was this trust in him that gave me the confidence to think that I could make a difference; that I could teach secondary school age children.

Faith and youthful energy conspired to get me the job! I then had to find somewhere to live, but quickly landed on my feet. The headmaster and his wife had two daughters around my age, who were living away from home. So the Buddles offered me one of their rooms. I would stay with them during the week, then return at weekends to the family home. This was now in Mount Salem, as Mas Charlie had saved enough money to purchase somewhere newly built through a government social housing scheme.

Having had a mere six weeks to transition from high-school student to pre-trained teacher, I approached the September term with great anticipation. Happily, I found myself adapting surprisingly well, quickly getting to grips with my new timetable and the work of preparing and delivering RE and PE lessons. It probably helped that I could easily see myself in the young people I was teaching. They were mainly from the surrounding rural area, and many came with a real desire to learn. Like my family, their families wanted them to do well, yet failed to understand the key role they might play by releasing them from household chores so they had time and space for their homework. My pupils appreciated my empathy and my youth, and we built a good rapport.

However, there were a few tough cookies. Looking back now, I suspect they weren't deliberately setting out to be rude and disruptive, and a couple were probably suffering from attention deficit hyperactivity disorder (ADHD). Though not yet eighteen, I found myself taking the initiative, deciding to undertake home visits in order to see what was happening with the disruptive students. Occasionally, these family meetings did give me a greater understanding. For example, in places of extreme poverty, there was anticipation that a student might 'hurry up' and leave school to enter the world of work and start contributing financially to the well-being of the family. It must have felt like quite a burden on young shoulders.

In contrast, I was thrilled about the freedom that being away from home offered, and largely enjoying my interactions with staff and students alike. Though I'd had practically no training for my job, I found myself exuding confidence, and as I showed no sign of being stressed, I was simply left to get on with things.

My self-assurance was sorely tested on one occasion, though, at an end-of-year party. A student who was a bit of a Jack the lad, and only a year or so younger than me, asked if I would dance and decided to try out the newest dub dance. I extricated myself from his hold as soon as I could – there was a lot of hip wriggling! – thankful that due to the colour of my skin, no one could see how embarrassed I was.

Another potentially more tragic incident remains vivid all these years later. It was the end of the school day, and children were pouring out onto the street as usual, when a cyclist rode straight into the crowd at great speed, seemingly not even trying to hit his brakes. A young boy was knocked flying onto the asphalt and seriously hurt. I took it upon myself to accompany him in a taxi to hospital, stayed with him until he was treated and then arranged for him to get back home.

Years later, on a blazing hot afternoon, I heard a voice calling after me as I wound my way through the streets of Montego Bay.

'Miss Rose, Miss Rose!'

I turned. A man I didn't recognise stood there.

'Don't you remember me, Miss Rose? I'm Robert Young. You helped me to hospital after the accident at school with the cyclist!'

The warmth of my smile assured him I recalled him well. After a few more words, during which he thanked me again, we went our separate ways, both touched and uplifted by the encounter.

I did not wish to overstay my time with the warm-hearted Buddles, and turned to the church to find alternative accommodation. Asking around, I discovered that a long-term member of St Francis Mission Church had a widowed brother who lived a ten-minute drive from the school and would be glad of some company. I called him as soon as I could and when we met, the vibes were great. He showed me around his spacious house and told me I could choose whichever room I wanted; he did not want any rent, simply for me to make myself at home. There was a hired helper, but I was welcome to cook, especially his favourite dish of liver gently dusted in seasoned flour and fried for a few minutes on both sides.

Mr Horace Whittingham was a gem. He was known locally as 'Busha Whitty', Busha being the name given to a person who owned or managed lots of farming land in the countryside (a sort of Lord of the Manor). Well known in the wider community and a Justice of the Peace (JP), Horace played a key role in the local parish church, St Luke's, and in due course we would spend lots of time discussing matters of faith and politics – national and international.

His beloved wife had died after a period of illness with cancer, and he spoke repeatedly of her and of his pride in his five adult children and his grandchildren. His kind heart led him to organise trips for the local children during the long school holidays – to the seaside or a local fun fair – and he was always ready to respond to the many and various needs of the community.

We soon adopted each other! He became my 'daddy' and I became his 'daughter'. You can imagine how deeply healing this was, given that my birth father, Joe, simply did not seem to have fatherhood in his DNA. Every morning, Horace would insist on dropping me off at school, and he'd come to collect me too if he was in the area, or if we were experiencing torrential rainfall. I saw in him someone who lived out his faith, and his wise advice and encouragement to pursue my dream was a real confirmation of my calling.

Believing such a great personality should not be without a close companion, I began to find myself playing with thoughts of seeing him remarried and had the bright idea of introducing him to my adopted (single) mom, Faye Jolly. The reality was, however, as Faye told me later, that Horace was still in love with his wife and no one could ever have stood in her shoes; but though it wasn't right for them to go down that road, they became firm friends. And so, at seventeen years of age, I had a mom and dad at last! They loved me unconditionally, and on the occasions we went out for a meal together, I was delighted to see their rapport. Horace's efforts to teach me to drive were a source of great amusement to us all, as he would mimic my impatience and have both Mommy and me in stitches.

With two powerful advocates now encouraging me into ministry, I made an application to the Diocese of Jamaica to train as a Church Army officer. The Church Army was started by a priest in the Church of England called Wilson Carlile. It began as a lay ministry, seeking to equip men and women to be evangelists. The three of us drove to Kingston for my interview, and I remember that Neville De Souza, who had just become Bishop of Jamaica having previously been Bishop of Montego Bay, and Captain Ernest Cousins, the pioneer and founder of Church Army Jamaica, were on the interview panel. Two brothers from St James's Deanery – Basil Smith and Revel Stoddart – were also being inter-viewed. Revel taught at Maldon Secondary School with me, while Basil was at a primary school in a neighbouring village. Both brothers attended the church that Daddy was part of. There was also a pair of twins, Yvonne and Jennifer Thomas, and they, along with Basil and me, were accepted for training. I returned to school at Maldon knowing that, in a few months, I would be leaving Jamaica for England to train as an evangelist.

Mom and Dad were thrilled for me. Aunt Pet, on the other hand, accepted the news without any real excitement. I think she was bewildered that I would not only be (fully) leaving home but actually leaving the country. When I told my father, there was just a nod of the head, as if to acknowledge what he'd heard. A man of few words, it was not surprising that he didn't engage with me on this; after all, he had never engaged with me on anything before. My mother similarly made little comment, but my beloved sister Shirley was bereft. Despite living at opposite ends of the country, we'd managed to stay very close and I knew we would miss each other dearly.

About a month before I was due to depart, a farewell service was organised at my church for Basil and me. I felt real joy that my vocation was seen and accepted by others, and I remember tearing up at the thought of the many friendships I would be leaving behind.

The flight would be departing from Kingston, so once more Dad and Mom were to drive me to the capital. They gave me a small copy of the Book of Common Prayer they had bought as a gift. Daddy had signed it, adding 'God is Love' from 1 John 4:8 for good measure. I didn't sleep very well that last night. Eventually, I got up and went through to Mom, who allayed my anxiety by praying with me. The memory of her mellifluous tones is still a comfort when I find myself confronted by challenging moments: 'Let the Lord's Spirit overshadow and guide you. Let him protect you and guide your travels with his great love and mercy.' Though my imagination was still running fairly wild into the early hours, things now seemed rather less daunting. And then, almost as soon as I'd dropped off to sleep, I found it was time to get up.

Captain Cousins and his wife Monica were there to greet us at the airport, along with Basil and the twins. By now, the buzz of excitement was palpable. At eighteen years old, I was leaving Jamaica for the first time to go to a completely new country, never having been on an aeroplane before. I made my way through immigration and suddenly felt completely overwhelmed. I was crying my eyes out.

'Can I go back out?' I begged. 'I just need to go back out!'

I ran and gave my dad a great big hug.

'You'd better get back in there, Rose!' And then such strange reassurance. In what seemed like the same voice I'd heard that night a while back in my dream: 'Everything will be well. You're not alone.' Dad's words were gentle, but the inexorable message was loud and clear. I was being called for ministry, away from the known to the unknown. I had promised God that I would be faithful.

I must put my trust in him.

5
STEPPING OUT

IT WAS LATE AUGUST. Although technically summer, the breeze immediately reminded me that I'd left the warmth and sunshine of Jamaica thousands of miles behind. I looked across at my fellow travellers and could see that they were aware of the difference in temperature too. Once through immigration, the four of us stayed close together. Perhaps our wide-eyed expressions gave us away, for soon we were approached by two members of the college staff, Sisters Stella Noons and Elizabeth Carr. Their smiles were welcoming; their grey pinafore dresses and white blouses – in contrast to the vibrant clothes we wore at home – gave a hint of what was to come.

Such drab brick buildings on the drive into London! At first, I assumed they must be factories, and you can imagine my disappointment when our Irish minibus driver, Dennis, informed me these were actually people's houses. Thinking of our beautiful, multicoloured homes with their individually styled verandas, I couldn't help but feel a little sad.

As the college hadn't yet reopened for the new academic year, we were taken to Brookfield House in Eccleston Square, close to the busy hub of Victoria Station. Venturing out for a walk in the mornings, I noticed that everywhere I looked people were rushing. Sometimes they were literally running.

A few days in, I plucked up the courage to ask a neatly dressed woman if there was a fire.

'A fire?' She looked around in some puzzlement. 'Why do you ask that?'

'Because you appear to be running,' came my naive response.

'I'm not running. I'm rushing to get the train – I only stopped because you looked lost!'

And with that she launched herself back into the heaving crowd. I remember thinking, *How strange! In Jamaica the train waits for you.*

When the time came to start college, Dennis returned to transport us to 27 Vanbrugh Park Road in Blackheath, near Greenwich Park, the location of the Wilson Carlile College of Evangelism. On arrival, a few students kindly came out to say hello and help with our luggage, and I later learned that the young man who carried my bags to my room was a certain Kenneth Wilkin. Sadly, I have no memory of him that day!

The college was set in beautiful surroundings. On the ground floor, there were classrooms, offices and two dining rooms. Separate wings housed male and female students, and the kitchen was to be found in the basement. We all settled in very quickly.

This was the term when the second years prepared for their annual assessment, and a couple of weeks after we'd arrived, a paper was sent round. We were to sign our name against the name of a person in that year we would like to pray for. I thought of three student brothers, as they were called, who always seemed to be together: Peter, Dennis and Martin. I wanted to pray for Peter, as I was aware he had a visual impairment, but by the time the list reached me Peter's name had already been taken, as had Dennis's and Martin's. My mind then turned to Kenneth Wilkin, who played the flute and sometimes the guitar at our chapel services. He seemed to have a real joy about him, as if making music was not just a thing he did, but something deep in his soul. I was pleased to find that no one else had chosen him, and when we happened to bump into each other in the administrative area a few days later, I said, 'You're Ken, aren't you?'

He nodded.

'I put my name against yours on the list. I'm praying for you!'

His eyes were warm and alive – they shone even then! 'Thank you. I'm pleased to hear it. I could do with your prayers.'

I'm sure he said more, but to be honest I only heard the first couple of words, so lost was I in delight at his Geordie accent! There was just something about Ken. He was unassuming and unpretentious, gentle and very down to earth. He seemed secure, never trying to prove himself or to dominate, and when we had a conversation, I felt I could simply be myself, without thinking about what I needed to say. Tall, well built and with the long hair that was obligatory in the seventies and early eighties, he had a thing about telling jokes. I liked him and really wanted to get to know him better.

The assessment period was quite an intense time for the whole college community, with even Dennis the driver, who was also the gardener, showing signs of greater care towards the students. The fact was that we were living a communal life with prayer at the heart of it.

On a practical level, that meant following a rota and taking turns to serve and clear up after meals. To this day, I'm still slightly ashamed to admit that when it was my turn to do the latter, I would make a beeline for the kitchen sink. I wanted to wash the dishes and cutlery my way – that is, the Jamaican way – cleaning and rinsing each item individually. The English students couldn't bear us Jamaican students being on washing-up duty. Everything took so much longer. But when they washed (swirled stuff around in the sink before dumping it on the draining board) and we dried, we'd often find ourselves removing large bits of food stuck to the utensils. My behaviour may have been a little un-Christlike – I did want to have my own way even though it caused others irritation – but we're all on a journey, and it's better to aim for progress rather than perfection.

Our beautiful chapel reminded me, from the outside, of an eagle about to fly. When you entered, the inspiring verses of Scripture inscribed on the four large windows at the corners of the building proved a major draw. Attending services was a major part of the daily rhythm of life, and everyone was expected to be there; there would be consequences come the time of your assessment if you habitually overslept. There was a daily Eucharist, Morning and Evening Prayer, and a College Eucharist on Wednesdays that those who lived off campus could attend with their families, booking meals too if they wished.

We spent half of each term in the college doing theory (such as Old and New Testament studies, doctrine, ethics, pastoral studies and church history). I have to admit that sitting in lectures was quite an experience for this girl from Montego Bay. It was all very new and sometimes disturbing to my spirit.

I'd grown up believing that the Bible was the Word of God; that is, the words it contained literally came direct from God! While I had no real idea as to *how* this might have happened, my vivid imagination had dreamed up all kinds of explanatory scenarios. One was that an angel had held someone's hand as they wrote the words the good Lord wanted us to know, beginning with Genesis and ending with Revelation. Now I was being told not only that there was no angel involved, but that several authors had written the Scriptures over many centuries and for different audiences. The real crunch came with the creation story. Imagine my horror when I discovered it wasn't real; that events simply didn't unfold as described at all! It was too much to take in, and on several occasions I went back to my room in tears.

One day, after I'd calmed down, I found myself replying out loud to my own question of 'Rose, what is the core of what you believe?'

'I believe in God. I believe that God created the world, and frankly I do not care whether he did it in seven days or over millions of years. I believe that God loves me and sent his Son to die for me. I believe that he rose again from the dead and that through him I have eternal life, beginning now, in Christ.'

Finding a way of expressing what was at the very heart of my faith was crucially important. I still believe profoundly what I verbalised and it has stood me in good stead, through the best and worst of times.

As a result of this wrestling, I suddenly found myself better able to handle lectures, and even began to look forward to them. I could view things more objectively and engage with what was being taught without feeling threatened. In short, I was beginning to relax and enjoy the process of learning.

For my first Christmas in England, I was invited by Ken to his parents' home. I later found out he'd told them I was a recently arrived Jamaican girl, and could I stay with them, he wondered, as they had a spare room? His sister, however, after seeing us walk in the park holding hands, ventured to remark, 'I think there's more to it than a lonely Jamaican girl with nowhere to go for the holidays!'

Ken was the image of his dad in many ways, with the same gentle personality. His birth mother had died, and his step-mother, Audrey, worked as a nurse at the local hospital, where Ken's dad was employed too. Neat, tidy and house proud, she reminded me very much of the women back home. The two of them were most warm and welcoming and I grew to love them. When I later met other members of the family, I decided I also loved the down-to-earth nature of northerners.

On one of my many trips to Ferryhill in County Durham, Audrey took me aside. 'Rose, I hope I'm not talking out of turn, but if he is anything like his dad, he's a good one.'

I hugged her and thanked her for the recommendation.

Back in Blackheath, part of the college experience involved students being sent off campus during the second half of each term. We visited various cities around the country on practical placements, such as prison chaplaincy, youth work, parish ministry, working in a women's, men's or youth hostel, or doing beach missions. My first placement was in a parish in Maidstone, which included a care home for the elderly. It was run by a Church Army officer, Captain Jim Etheridge, who was my supervisor, and my time was split between the care home and the church.

One evening, I found myself helping an elderly man get ready for bed. I tucked him in, kissed him on the forehead and said goodnight, but as I made my way towards the door, he began to cry.

I rushed back. 'What's the matter?' I asked.

He raised tear-filled eyes to mine. 'No one has ever tucked me in and kissed me since my mother did, when I was a little boy.'

I felt moved to hug him again and sat with him for a while longer as he reminisced about the time he served in the Second World War. In my prayers that night, I gratefully thanked God for his courage and the sacrifices he and his friends had made while in service.

Another of my assignments in Maidstone was partnering with a teenager on door-to-door visits – usually a pretty uneventful activity. However, on one fateful day, when the door we'd knocked on opened, a large hairy dog came bounding towards us. I speedily grabbed my companion, shoved her in front of me and then froze. Having been bitten as a child, I'm petrified of dogs even to this day, which can be a real challenge in parish ministry, where one is still expected to make home visits! Luckily, this youngster had no such fear, though she well understood mine and assured me my heart-felt apology was not needed. I still can't think of this incident without great embarrassment.

Presenting something of a contrast were the children's beach missions in Clacton, with Sister Peggy Boynes. When they're on holiday, parents are generally more than happy to have their children looked after for an hour or so. We sang short songs, such as 'My God is so Big, so Strong and so Mighty' and 'Love is a Flag Flying High from the Castle of My Heart', and the children loved joining in with the actions. The Bible stories were also dramatised, which created a buzz as everyone wanted to get in on the action. I enjoyed myself as much as the children did, and I'm sure they loved that we were also having fun.

A more testing but equally rewarding placement took me to Leeds, where the Church Army worked with the disenfranchised and homeless. We fed them a hot meal in the evenings, and those who slept in the crypt had a cooked breakfast the next morning. The year was 1980, and the notorious mass murderer known as the Yorkshire Ripper was still at large. Peter Sutcliffe had killed thirteen women and was charged with the attempted murder of a further seven. I recall being on edge as I walked around after dusk in Leeds. After all, black women numbered among those he had murdered, so I could not afford to let down my guard. I was staying at a women's hostel, checking the doors repeatedly each time I came and went, to make sure they were properly locked. I was taking no chances.

There were other moments that made Leeds memorable for me. Relinquishing the warmth of my homeland seemed worth it when I experienced my first snowfall! I felt like a small child in a sweet shop as I ran around trying to catch those beautiful feathery flakes. The folks back in Jamaica heard at length about just how magical it had been.

Whenever I was away from the college, I was supervised by men and women who had a real passion for the gospel and believed in passing this on. During one placement on lay ministry, Canon Ivor Smith-Cameron really inspired me in terms of growing disciples and intentionally equipping the laity to live out their faith daily so the Church could thrive. Coming from a diocese where we were very short of priests, I immediately recognised that more needed to be done to emphasise the priesthood of all believers. I assisted Canon Ivor in delivering some teaching modules on leadership and, invigorated by this and the experience gained, felt drawn to make equipping the laity the focus of my future ministry.

Over the years, receiving encouraging notes from Canon Ivor was very special, because I always knew he was praying for me. Approximately three and a half months before he died at the age of ninety-three in March 2024, I visited him in hospital. His eyes were closed.

'Hello, Ivor,' I whispered.

His eye-lids lifted.

'This is Rose. Do you remember me?'

'Rose Hudson-Wilkin? Yes!' he exclaimed.

I was so touched and thrilled.

In January 1982 I came of age. I had not discussed my existence before college with anyone, and my fellow students would probably have been greatly surprised to hear that I'd never celebrated a birthday in my life. Now, at twenty-one, having survived the challenges of childhood, I found I was no longer hurting. I could look at my scars and be aware of how I came by them without experiencing the old pain.

I felt not only happy but joyful, and I wanted to share that joy with others.

I convinced Charles Hutchins, the principal, to let me cook for the whole college. I'm not sure if he consulted the rest of the staff, but permission was given anyway. I was thrilled that some of the other Jamaican students were happy to assist, and overexcited to be preparing a meal full of Jamaican flavour for all to enjoy. We made sure that the chicken was well seasoned and, as we would have done back home, we left it overnight for the seasoning to soak into the meat. The next day the aroma of that baked chicken could be smelled from afar. Accompanied by rice and a variety of salads, the meal was the main event in a happy, successful evening. I even got to dance with the principal! The icing on the cake, however, was that Ken – who had completed his three years and returned to the north of England to work in Hartlepool – came back specially to help me celebrate.

I was near to finishing my three-year course too, and my classmates and I were finding our final assessment very stressful. We had to make sure our academic work had been completed and handed in on time, that reflections with regard to our practical placements had been written up, and we had to demonstrate that any projects we had embarked on had been completed, with the evidence handed in to our assessors. They then interviewed us, read reports from the academic staff, and listened to our tutors and placement supervisors speak about our overall performance. It felt like being placed under a microscope. I was very glad to be prayed for by the students in the year below!

Sadly, as in all places of education, not everyone passed, and during my time at the college I was aware of one student who made the decision to remain in England, despite being told they would be given a pass for their assessment if they returned to Jamaica. I was shocked. Jamaica needed the best! If the student had not achieved what was required to be admitted to the office of evangelist in the UK, they should not be bumped up simply if they went home.

This evidence of double standards prompted me once again to challenge the status quo. I've always been very good at getting my point across when I'm fired up. I allow myself to be led, not just by my heart, but by my gut, which I regard as a special inner spirit. I need to be on the side of justice and will not hold back from speaking truth to power when necessary, though I must say I am not afraid to reflect on the nature of 'my truth' and to make changes if necessary.

My protest was not appreciated. Seemingly I was rocking the boat. And it did not help my own cause, for on the one hand I was writing to the Bishop of Jamaica in protest and on the other I was asking to return to serve, not in St Francis Mission in Glendevon, like so many other returning Church Army officers did, but in pioneering lay ministry work.

The day of our commissioning finally arrived, and we gathered in Southwark Cathedral for the service, with the Most Revd Robert Runcie, the then Archbishop of Canterbury, officiating. I was glad to have some family there: Uncle George and his wife Linnett, as well as Ken's parents. Captain Ernest Cousins, who had been one of my interviewers at the beginning, was also in attendance, having come over from Jamaica to celebrate the Church Army's centenary. It was all very moving, and after the official photographs had been taken, I felt quite tearful. A part of me was excited to be returning home, but there was also sadness, because I would be leaving behind friends I'd made over the last three years, not to mention a very special one who had become important to me.

My mind flitted with all sorts of possibilities, though the truth was that I had no sense of when I might return to England. However, I remembered the old saying, 'If God will, the future will all be possible,' and felt reassured. God had a plan for my heart as well as my ministry. All was in his hands.

6
BACK TO MONTEGO BAY

TOWARDS THE END OF MY COURSE, I'd been given a poster by one of my tutors. Although it had been picked at random from a pile, its message struck such a chord that I felt someone was speaking directly to me about the next stage of my life: 'Do not go where the path leads. Go where there is no path and leave a trail.' But how to reconcile such a call with my burgeoning feelings for Ken ...

On my arrival in England, I'd had no thoughts of finding one special person. However, when young people are put together in a residential setting, it's fairly probable that attractions will form. I really liked how relaxed and easy going Ken seemed to be. For his part, he probably thought I was a bit strange, because I would never join everyone in the pub for a drink. My mind unhappily associated English pubs with Jamaican rum bars, and although I came to appreciate that the culture is completely different, even today my idea of going out does not include the pub.

I was, however, always glad to take part in our communal trips to Greenwich Park nearby. After a while, I began to notice that I looked out for Ken at mealtimes and in chapel, even if I didn't go and sit with him. I also noticed that I missed him when he was not around.

I remember being both troubled and confused about this development, because there was someone I'd been interested in back in Jamaica. We mainly met at deanery youth events, and as seventeen-year-olds without a road map of what this should look like, or indeed feel like, made no promises to each other. But there was the assumption that when I returned to Jamaica we would resume our relationship. And now someone in the UK had caught my attention. And yes, Ken was white! I had no idea whether our attraction would lead anywhere or indeed if I wanted it to. What was unmistakable was that it was both emotional and mutual.

I had, of course, stayed in touch with family and friends over the previous three years, and my anxiety about being pulled away from Ken was tempered by my longing to be with my sister and adopted parents once more. I'd missed them so much. As it was not easy to phone, I'd always been eager for the post to arrive, and luckily they wrote to me regularly. Their precious letters contained news of Dad, back in the hills, and of Mom at the mission church in Glendevon. I could easily recognise the sender: Dad had beautiful flowing handwriting; Mom's looked much more intense and laboured.

Of course, I loved hearing from my sister Shirley. As well as telling me about what was happening in her own life, she shared news of the family in Kingston too. Communication from my birth mother was minimal. I do recall receiving a letter in which she told me she had it on good authority that people wanted to harm me. I found this disturbing and shared it with my tutor, Terry Henderson, who listened attentively before suggesting we pray together about the matter. Thankfully, this meant I could park my mother's message and not carry it around with me. Aunt Pet didn't write, but Juney would drop me the occasional note. In short, the pain of leaving England was lessened a little by knowing I'd been missed, and that people were waiting for me.

A stopover in Miami, Florida on the way back to Jamaica also helped. I was travelling with Basil Smith, and he'd agreed to visit his sister, also called Shirley, for a couple of days. This would be my first visit to the USA and on applying for a visa to facilitate the stopover, I received the coveted multiple-indefinite one. Having this visa was a big, big deal at the time.

Shirley, Basil's sister, met us at the airport with such genuine warmth and welcome that we became firm friends, notwithstanding a considerable age gap. We were only parted forty years later when I officiated at her requiem mass in Miami.

Finally, back on Jamaican soil, I was overjoyed to be enfolded by Dad and Mom in a loving embrace. Yet I was immediately aware that things had changed. I'd left Jamaica a teenager and returned a woman. And not just any woman, but a Church Army evangelist, ready to make good her promise to God to serve him in ministry. I was buzzing with excitement.

The Bishop of Jamaica may not have appreciated my intervention regarding some of the decisions being made at the college, but he had responded to my request to be involved in pioneering lay ministry work. Rather than returning to the church that had nurtured me, I was invited to take up a newly formed post in the county of Cornwall, one of Jamaica's three regional counties (the other two being Middlesex and Surrey).

Cornwall itself had five parishes: St James, Hanover, Westmoreland, Trelawny and St Ann. My task was to engage the laity – the army of people who did all they could to keep the show on the road. I devised and delivered training programmes for youth leaders, Sunday school teachers and lay readers, and those in leadership within the Women's Auxiliary, the Mother's Union and the Brotherhood of St Andrew. My strategy was to get to know the key people, develop an understanding of what it was they did, and then listen as they told me the kind of support they needed.

Working out of the Bishop of Montego Bay's office was helpful, as it enabled the bishop and me to communicate regularly about how the job was going. I'm still in touch with individuals who attended the workshops I led, many of whom have gone on to make a substantive contribution to leadership in the life of their local church. Only recently it filled me with deep joy to hear a lay person tell the current bishop that he became a reader because of my encouragement all those years ago. The occasion was a special anniversary evensong at the Cathedral of St Jago de la Vega in Spanish Town, to mark the 200th anniversary of the Diocese of Jamaica and the Cayman Islands. It was a privilege to be asked to contribute to the life of the diocese again.

Back in the 1980s, my work as the lay training officer took me all over the county. It was absorbing and fulfilling, and although I could not ignore my longing to serve God in a different role, I remembered my promise to be faithful and settled in well. During that first year, Ken flew to Jamaica to pay me a visit. He stayed with our mutual friends Carl and Joan Ramsay. Ken and Carl had been in the same year at college, and Carl was now in charge at St Francis Mission Church in Glendevon. Together we showed Ken around the island, and I also introduced him to my family, including the adopted wing.

The fact was that the neighbourhood where I was now living was far removed from those I'd known previously in Kingston and Montego Bay. On the outskirts of the latter, wealthy Coral Gardens sat alongside a similar community called Ironshore. In both these areas, many returning residents had built extravagant houses that were quite beyond their realistic needs, such as they would have loved – but could not afford – to own in the UK. It was, I admit, delightful to have a home there, but that never stopped me appreciating where I'd come from and the connections I still had in those places.

On meeting Aunt Pet, Ken was assailed with, 'Did Rose tell you dat I raise her?'

'No,' he replied.

And before I could jump in, Aunt Pet piped up again, 'Shame on you, Rose!'

A wave of irritation made me bite back in kind. 'Ken, you know I've told you that I was brought up by my aunt.'

His response still makes me smile: 'I thought she was saying something about a razor!'

Rather than obtuseness, it had been a classic cultural misunderstanding. I proceeded to interpret Aunt Pet's patois.

However, my aunt had clearly thought I'd not shared with Ken the role she had played in my life. How far from the truth she was. I'd never hidden my humble beginnings from him. The fact was that before I left the UK, Ken had given me an engagement ring! We seemed to have arrived at the decision that we really cared about each other and would seek to explore what it might mean to be together; the affection we'd felt at college had matured into something more real and tangible. When I got back to Jamaica, we spoke at least once a week, and there were many letters too. During Ken's fortnight in Jamaica, we found ourselves earnestly musing over a date for our wedding in 1983, the following year.

Ken met with the Bishop of Jamaica to discuss the possibility of a job after we got married. The bishop told him that although he couldn't make such a promise at that point, he'd be willing to revisit the matter when Ken returned. This more or less made our decision for us. We wanted our relationship to work, and knew that the physical distance between us was challenging. So while Ken made plans to return the following year, I carried on working to develop my ministry of equipping the laity and, with the great support of Carl and Joan, took on the new and somewhat demanding role of wedding-planner-in-chief.

7
TILL DEATH DO US PART

OVER THE YEARS, my inability to recollect Ken ever proposing to me has become something of a recurring conversation.

'Well, how did we come to be married then?' he'd ask.

'I have no idea.'

Ken would pretend to be offended that I didn't remember his big romantic gesture.

Refusing to back down, I'd challenge him, 'OK, so when did it happen and what did you say?'

He'd retort, 'If you can't remember, then I'm not telling you!'

With this in mind, you can imagine how touched I was to discover on the occasion of our twenty-fifth wedding anniversary that Ken planned to propose to me all over again. We renewed our vows at a service with gathered friends and family, including Carl, who (as you'll discover) was Ken's best man, and their fellow student at college, the Revd Stephen Caple. At the appointed time during the reception, Ken shared our story, causing much amusement, and then not only reproposed to me down on one knee, but sang – with musical back-up – Barry White's 'You're My First, My Last, My Everything'! Several heartwarming speeches followed.

But though my first proposal may have been unrecallable, the marriage ceremony itself was an entirely different matter …

I wanted a simple and affordable wedding – certainly nothing that would leave me in debt afterwards – and as Carl and Joan had an eye for detail, I was glad to bounce some of my practical plans off them. Others rallied round, including Everald and Jean Rose. Everald was the Deputy Superintendent of Police in the Montego Bay region and Jean was a member of the congregation. They generously offered us the use of their home for the wedding reception. There was a sticking point, however: although the guests would be mingling outdoors, Jean's dining table, where the bride and groom would be seated, could not be taken out into the garden! As I was incredibly grateful for their generosity and not in the mood for an argument, I smiled and said that would be just fine.

Mom offered two cases of chicken and my friend Andy agreed to have it cooked and delivered. Dad was to be both my driver and the father who gave me away. I made sure to let my birth father, Joe, know that he was most definitely invited to the wedding, but that I wanted Dad to give me away. It would not have been right to tell him what was in my heart – that Mr Whittingham was more of a dad to me than he had ever been. It's difficult to guess, as he was not a man for showing emotion, if my father Joe was disappointed that he would not be walking me down the aisle. We just did not have the kind of relationship that meant I could ask how he felt about my decision. But whatever his deeper feelings, I suspect he was relieved to avoid the public scrutiny such a role would involve. And, as things turned out, he played a part in a different way …

My mother had offered a goat – a live goat – and we transported the animal in the (slightly ajar) boot of our car from Spanish Town to the slaughterhouse in Montego Bay, only to discover on arrival that there was a strike on. Joe stepped up to the plate, slaughtering and preparing the goat for us – a role he was infinitely more comfortable with than anything else wedding related. There would be two dishes made from it: the head, feet and entrails would be used for mannish water, a delicacy considered to be an aphrodisiac that would be served at the start of the reception; the rest would be curried and served with rice as one of the main meal options.

Ken was due to arrive at Montego Bay airport two weeks before the wedding. A friend of mine who worked there invited me into an area I would not normally have had access to, allowing me to get a first glimpse of my husband-to-be alighting from the plane. Having not seen him in several months, I felt somewhat apprehensive. It didn't seem fair to tell him that I was wondering if it would all work out. After all, he'd left everything for me, all his possessions bundled into just two suitcases in readiness for being married and settling down in Montego Bay. There was not even a job guaranteed for him at this stage.

Watching Ken carefully descend the aircraft steps, I became aware that the thudding of my heart was due less to passion than to sheer terror. The moustache he had grown made him seem unfamiliar, and suddenly my chest was threatening to explode. I ran out of the room. I needed air. I needed to think. The enormity of what I was about to embark on overwhelmed me. Was it the right thing? We were from such very different cultural backgrounds. Would we still feel the same, away from the confines of the Church Army college?

The decision we'd made to be together seemed, at that moment, to be an event in a far distant past. Were we simply following through because we couldn't see an alternative? Or were we getting married because we were still in love with each other? As the questions tumbled around my mind, I knew I had to keep them to myself. Introducing doubt into the mix might result in things taking a disastrous turn, and that would affect Ken more than me. I gulped in big breaths of the hot outside air. Could this truly be 'happy ever after' for us?

When Ken eventually cleared customs, we hugged, and even as we embraced each other I realised that many of my questions were unanswerable. As so often before, I needed to step out of my comfort zone and embark on a journey of faith. Nonetheless, as we drove back to the Ramsays' home in Glendevon, unspeakable fears continued churning around inside me.

Over the next few days, there was plenty to do, including collecting Ken's parents, Matthew and Audrey, his aunt Ann and her husband Mike, his sister Valerie and her husband Eric, and his step-sister Susan, who'd brought along one of her friends for company. All of them were staying with me, so it was a full house.

A day or two before the wedding, it was agreed we'd go for evening drinks at the nearby Holiday Inn. I decided to take the men folk first to see the venue for the reception, and while I chatted to Jean, Mr Rose was delighted to share some of the contents of his drinks cabinet with his male visitors. However, when they seemed to be lingering over their drinks, I pointed out that the rest of the family were waiting for us to return.

It transpired Mr Rose had clear ideas about who should wear the trousers in a marriage.

'A bird can't fly on one wing,' he muttered disapprovingly.

I felt it bode well for Ken and me when his dad Matthew replied, 'We're going to have both wings clipped if we don't get back soon!'

It turned out that the ladies were beginning to wonder where on earth we'd got to, but although we were late, everyone had a good time. Being with Ken and his family that evening was reassuring. I remember thinking of the Ken who had played the flute beautifully and this, along with Matthew setting Mr Rose straight, made me feel everything would be all right. After all, it was a mixture of music and forthrightness that had brought us together under God.

On the morning of the wedding, I discovered Ken hadn't yet sorted out the honeymoon. I was not impressed, but in my new state of calm I focused on doing what I could to make things happen. Eventually, with the advice of Mom, we booked into Seawinds, which was then a German-owned hotel in Montego Bay.

Valerie (Ken's sister) was my bridesmaid. It felt good to be wearing a dress I had made myself, albeit with a bit of help from my friend Frieda who lived nearby. The style was one-sleeved, simple and straight. Another friend, Jojo, had done my hair, and I carried a single red rose. Less was more and I was happy.

My step-father, Vincent Bernard, had died back in 1973 during an altercation with a tenant. Ten years later, it was my mother's new partner, Keith, who drove her and all my younger siblings down from Kingston, though I don't recall if he came into the church service. I do remember my sister Shirley's beautiful face smiling up at me. Her husband Peat was there, along with Aunt Pet, Mas Charlie, all the cousins I'd grown up with, and Aunt Lou and her husband Ralph. My Sunday school teachers Annette Mellish and Mrs Kerr came. Some of the people I worked with were also in attendance, including the head of the Church Army, Captain Cousins, and his wife Monica, Sister Norma Thompson, and the Bishop of Montego Bay, Alfred Reid, and his wife Gloria. Former Church Army officers Bishop Harold Daniels and his wife Canon Judith Daniels, who served at St Francis, and some of the local clergy, added to the spiritual colour of our special day, and with the diocesan bishop, the Right Revd Ernest deSouza officiating, we felt truly blessed. The veritable icing on the cake was that Charles Hutchins, the principal of the Church Army college in London, flew out to Jamaica especially to preach the sermon.

As I look back, I'm conscious that my wedding is the only time, subsequent to my mother's departure for England when I was two, that I remember my birth parents being in the same space. How I wish I'd been able to get them to hold a conversation! I'd have loved to hear Joe and Eunice speaking to one another, maybe reflecting on the two children they shared, or even seizing the moment to say to Shirley and me something like, 'Well done for making it through.' But I knew even then that that was wishful thinking. After all, they didn't really know us and had never truly made any effort to do so. It may well be that they essentially lacked the capacity to engage emotionally with their children.

As we were getting ready to leave the church for the reception, Joe told me he wanted to head back home. Maybe he was finding the day too much to cope with. Certainly he knew no one apart from immediate family members and would have been far outside his comfort zone. I reluctantly made arrangements for him to be driven back to Rosemount – the only slight blight on an otherwise joyful day, when I truly relished having such a breadth of family, friends and colleagues around me.

Ken and I opened the floor as we danced to 'Endless Love' by Lionel Richie and Diana Ross – one of my favourite songs – and we followed that with another from Lionel, 'Lady, I'm Your Knight in Shining Armour'.

During the course of the evening, the Revd Dennis Kerr gave the toast to my family. He had been the Church Army captain leading at St Francis Mission during the first part of my high school years. He was aware of my life story, and when I preached at his funeral back in Montego Bay thirty-six years later, the kind and generous words he offered were echoing through my mind still.

My brother-in-law Eric toasted Ken's family, and the principal of the local teacher-training college, Mr Simon Clarke, acted as the master of ceremonies. It was he who offered Ken some mannish water when we arrived at the reception. I still remember Ken's reaction after having had most of the soup and then finding a jawbone with teeth intact looking back at him from the cup. It was the last time he had that kind of soup! Mannish water would be for ever off his menu, and I do wonder whether the incident contributed to him embracing vegetarianism later in life.

Knowing I had to make several trips to drive Ken's family the short distance back to my home, I didn't drink any alcohol apart from a couple of sips with the toasts. Walking back would not have been an option. Although we were in what could have been described as a posh neighbourhood, being held up at gunpoint was a real possibility.

At the end of the evening, when everyone was safely home, Ken and I drove to Seawinds to begin our honeymoon.

We had agreed beforehand that we would have only two days at the hotel, because with Ken's folk being in Jamaica it made sense to spend time with them. They thoroughly enjoyed seeing a number of sights, including Dunns River Falls in Ocho Rios and the infamous Doctor's Cave Beach in Montego Bay, and it was with sadness that we finally said farewell at the airport. But I had to get back to work and Ken needed to have that long-awaited meeting with our diocesan bishop about getting a job.

The bishop and Ken discussed a role that would see him driving out into the countryside to officiate in Cornwall Mountain and Chester Castle. Both were rural churches with humble church folk and Ken was in for a real culture shock. A classic example was when he was asked, 'How is the mistress?' Ken spluttered and stammered until he realised that they were actually asking about me, his wife!

Other things took some getting used to, including the retired police officer being called Cawpi (Corporal), the local tailor Tailey, and the postman (yes!) Postie. But the most important lesson we learned from this time was just what generosity could mean. Every visit to the local village would result in a car boot full of fruit and vegetables that we would distribute to friends and family.

In Jamaica, as in the UK, cars are driven on the left, but that's where the similarity ends. Many drivers pay no attention to the rules of the road, and I always worried when Ken left for the countryside. I would monitor his journey back, and if he was not home at a certain time, my imagination would simply run away with me. On one occasion, I'd begun calling the police stations en route to find out if there had been any accidents, and I was just being put through to the local A&E department when he walked in. I should really have had more faith, because Ken is an exceptionally careful driver, who always stays within the speed limit. Even now, if I ask him to go a bit faster, he'll happily remark that he's never had a speeding ticket – unlike you-know-who.

I learned pretty early on in our relationship that food shopping together was not a good idea, as it involved Ken carefully examining every item of produce before doing a comparison price check with all the other brands on the shelf. Shopping for clothing was no less challenging, as whenever I picked something up he'd ask, 'Do you really need it?' It used to drive me crazy. Forty years on, shopping is still not something we do together, and I often encourage couples to get to know the irritation points in their relationship and do those things together less frequently – or remove them from the agenda completely.

Our three years in Jamaica were wonderful. However, Ken was beginning to feel a call to ordination, and as we talked things over, he shared his conviction that this would mean returning to England: he didn't feel it would be fair for the Jamaican Church to use its resources to train him for the priesthood.

The Church Army kindly put us in touch with a parish priest in the south London district of Tulse Hill, the Revd John Sentamu. This was the very same drum-playing John who was to become Area Bishop of Stepney, then Bishop of Birmingham, before being appointed England's first black Archbishop of York. Along with his wife, Margaret, John was originally from Uganda. He'd been a high court judge who'd stepped up to challenge the notorious Idi Amin (president from 1971 to 1979), and been beaten and imprisoned as a consequence. With the assistance of the then Bishop of Lichfield, Keith Sutton, who'd worked in Uganda, the couple and their family migrated to the UK, where John studied theology at Cambridge and answered a call to ordained ministry.

Ken and John liaised over the phone – this being long before the advent of Zoom and Teams – and plans were made for us to return to England in April 1985. Ken would be employed as a Church Army officer, and I would have a supportive non-stipendiary Church Army role. Just at that point – because there wasn't enough going on in our lives! – we decided to prepare to start a family.

Saying goodbye to all I knew and loved in Jamaica for a second time was bittersweet. Every farewell party left me feeling that I was really only going to be on loan to Britain; that I was truly a daughter of Jamaica and my absence would be with everyone's blessing. This generous gifting of love meant that instead of fearing the unknown, I was filled with a sense of well-being and happy anticipation of whatever lay ahead. Mommy and Daddy continued to encourage me, reassuring me that they would keep in touch, just as they had the last time I was in England.

And so, furnished with two suitcases each, Ken and I left Jamaica that spring, knowing that a brand new chapter was opening in our lives. As the plane took off, I heard Mom and Dad's words ringing in my ears above the roar of the engines: 'We love you. We're proud of you. Go well.'

8
IT'S COLD!

ARRIVING IN THE UK, I was struck again by the change in temperature. This time, though, it was not simply a case of adapting to a refreshing breeze. I was cold. Possibly heading to the north of England first to see Ken's family added to my impression of physical coldness (it was only April, after all), but I think I was also becoming more aware of the way typical British reserve could add a chilliness to human interaction.

That said, the warmth of our reception in Tulse Hill was never in doubt. John and Margaret welcomed us with open arms, gladly helping us to settle into our new home and work. As the Church Army evangelist, Ken would be running holiday clubs among other things – he quickly became Captain Ken to the children – and doing work on the local estates. I too would be fully engaged in the life of the parish, supporting Ken and preaching when called upon to do so. It was an exciting time, as the primary focus was on mission, and we had an abundance of students and young people, some with a passion for this work, some to be drawn in, including those at the attached primary school.

Today, many going forward for ordination training speak of wanting to be a pioneer minister. Well, without shouting about it, or naming it as such, John Sentamu and the team quietly and to great effect pioneered new ways of being church for the whole parish.

As Ken's desire for ordination was encouraged and supported by John, the process was kickstarted with the Diocesan Director of Ordinands (DDO). Before long, Ken had been recommended for training and enrolled on the part-time programme of the Southwark Ordination Course (SOC). And, as we'd so carefully planned, we began the work of starting a family.

This turned out to be not a purely pleasurable experience, for after exploratory surgery we discovered that I was not ovulating, and it was also determined that Ken had a low sperm count! We were lucky to benefit from this early medical intervention, but though some incidents did have comic overtones, such as Ken cycling to the hospital in haste with his sperm samples, this was not an easy time for us. We knew it was a matter best committed to prayer within the church, and that if God willed it we would be blessed with an addition to the family.

Some months later, I woke up as Ken was making breakfast. It seemed that burnt toast was on the menu, and found myself feeling rather nauseous. As the day dragged on and the nausea became worse, I decided to call the doctor for an appointment. After a brief examination, he pronounced that I was pregnant. Wow! I was so excited at this wonderful news that I actually hugged him (so much for protocol!). What we had committed to God was becoming a reality, and our much-prayed-for baby was on its way.

During my prenatal visits to King's College Hospital, I was attended by a midwife called Shirley Samuels. She and my sister not only shared the same first and last names; my sister was also a practising midwife in Jamaica at the time!

On the afternoon of 2 August 1986, I began to feel a slight tightening of the abdominal area, which indeed turned out to be the beginning of labour. I spoke with the hospital, but as my waters had not yet broken and the contractions were few and far between, they discouraged me from going in until late evening. By that stage, the contractions were still half an hour apart, but it was clear my anxiety levels were rising!

I was admitted on a rather busy night. It appeared there was only a skeleton staff on duty, and Ken and I were left by ourselves as the midwife attending me (not the Shirley I knew) assisted other women who were also waiting for a much-anticipated baby to arrive. At one point, she disappeared just as I was having a contraction and I remember screaming out, 'Everybody's leaving me!' The calm rejoinder came from Ken that he wasn't going anywhere. Certainly, he was physically in the room, but as he kept nodding off his presence wasn't particularly reassuring. I'd have to thump him at intervals and roar, 'Stay awake with me! You're not allowed to fall asleep while I'm in agony!'

After several more checks by the midwife, I was still not dilated enough, and we were told that the best way to proceed was for my waters to be broken manually. The medics would wait for me to have a contraction before cutting me with scissors to help the baby's delivery. Though pretty high on gas and air by this point, I was understandably filled with dread.

I'm sharing this detailed account of my experience giving birth because it has made a real difference to my reading of the Scripture, where Jesus is in the Garden of Gethsemane. Aware of what the coming days will bring, he invites his most trusted disciples and friends to pray and keep vigil with him. But overwhelmed by the enormity of unfolding events, they fall asleep. Jesus, in agony, asks, 'Could you not stay awake with me one hour?' (Matthew 26:40).

What a weight our Lord carried as he approached Golgotha. What a weight women carry as they prepare to bring the next generation into the world. It is no ordinary feat, and we too need to know that there are companions along the way, willing to journey with us, to stay awake with us in the pain of labour, and to share the joy with us as we welcome each new miracle, each new life. Mother Julian of Norwich's insight that God chose to be our Mother in all things certainly takes on an added poignancy when you have given birth.

Returning my thoughts to the early hours of 3 August 1986, I can still feel and hear the crunch of the scissors doing its work (to prevent tearing, I was told) in the midst of a contraction, as it was supposed to be less painful then! What an assault on the female body, even if the intentions were good. However, one more big push and Amanda Ruth finally decided she was in a rush to enter this world and came flying out across the bed. My firstborn!

Weighing in at 7 lb 4 oz, the baby was in good health, which made being awake as I was stitched up easier to bear. Ken headed home (exhausted!), leaving the two of us on the delivery ward, and at one point Amanda yawned. That was another 'Wow!' moment and I responded by saying out loud: 'Oh my God, she has a tongue!' What had I expected? Examining her body, I found myself continuously thanking God that everything was as it should be.

On hearing of our new arrival, John Sentamu transported all the flowers that had been in church that Sunday morning to the hospital. My room looked like a florist's shop. When we were discharged a few days later, those flowers came home with us. Ken carefully dried some of the petals and we treasure them even now.

Though I had no blood family to guide me in this new parenting role, I was blessed with adopted mothers and sisters in the congregation; women who made it their mission to ensure that despite being far from my country of birth, I had all the support a young mother could possibly need. In the first few days, they brought me Jamaican delicacies so I didn't have to cook. Ken and I decided to choose Amanda's godparents from among the congregation – three people who we knew would faithfully pray for our daughter – and although we are long gone from the parish, I am pleased to say they are still in touch with her.

Our daughter was an adorable, easy-going child, and when she was six months old I was glad to take her to Jamaica to meet my family and friends. The only tears on the aircraft were during take-off and landing. We had a wonderful time.

When we were out walking in town, Amanda would be strapped to me. The scarcity of pavements meant there was no point in taking a pushchair, and when there *were* pavements, 'higglers' filled them, hustling with each other to sell their wares. Ordinary folk on the street assumed, due to the difference in skin tone, that I was my child's hired nanny and addressed me as such. To be honest, I was rather amused by it all. On one occasion, a friend was driving us to church and her six-month-old just wouldn't settle. With my friend's permission, I decided to breastfeed him. It clearly did not bother him that I was not his real mother. He gladly drank his fill of breast milk all the way there.

Hannah Marie, our second child, was born in March 1988, while I was going through the diaconate approval process (that's for another chapter). I was very lucky to be able to breastfeed both my girls from birth to ten months, and stopped on each occasion because they had teeth that could do damage! Neither baby liked me to be talking to others while I was feeding them and they expressed their disapproval by biting down painfully on my nipple. That was the cue to move them on to a cup of cow's milk and introduce them to hard food. Where I came from, hard food meant eating more than just Irish potato (potato as we eat it in the UK, but called Irish potato to distinguish it from sweet potato), so crushed yams and bananas became part of their diet. Luckily, we lived a short distance from Brixton market, where we could access just about everything that was sold in Jamaica.

Our family would eventually be completed with Jamie, our adopted son, who joined us in June 1994 a couple of months before his fourth birthday.

By then, England no longer felt cold. Thanks to my ministry, I'd been able to bring into my life here the love and colour of my home country.

9
TRY, TRY AND TRY AGAIN

IT WAS WHILE AMANDA was still a toddler that I began to explore the call to ordination I had heard when I was just fourteen. Women were now being ordained to the diaconate (office of deacon) in England; nevertheless, my time with the DDO was a rather uncomfortable experience. There was no sense of 'We have very few people from a minority ethnic background' (they could be counted on one hand with space left over), 'so let's see if this person before us is right for this ministry.' And the fact that I was a wife and mother didn't help my cause. Time and time again I heard the same refrain: 'Why do you think this is the right path for you? Shouldn't you be at home looking after your husband and daughter?' I would reply, 'My husband is perfectly capable of looking after himself and had I not thought about how I would take care of my daughter, I would not have progressed with this discernment process.'

Despite support from Bishop Peter Selby and John Sentamu, the wheels ground slowly. So slowly, in fact, that when the DDO finally got in touch with me about restarting the process, I was pregnant with child number two. Internally I staged mock interviews with myself, trying to work out how to let them know this after they'd been so disparaging the last time. The hamster wheel of anxiety had a field day in my brain.

Maybe they would re-interview me before my pregnancy showed.

Maybe they would ask a different question this time.

On and on it went.

Unsurprisingly, by the time a letter finally arrived, I was just two weeks away from giving birth.

Professor Leslie Houlden was the person I was asked to see, and he was refreshingly gracious and respectful, despite my quip of, 'I hope your midwifery skills are intact, as I am told one can go into labour two weeks either side of one's delivery date!' He never once asked me how I would manage to look after my family while being engaged in ministry. Instead, we talked theology – Leslie was a former principal of Cuddesdon Theological College – and he left me feeling that my calling was indeed a realistic one.

However, the process had taken us up to the end of Ken's training and, as there were no appropriate curacies going in Southwark, I would need to pursue ordination elsewhere. Before we could move, Hannah's delivery date was upon us.

And then she was two weeks overdue. An examination showed that the cord was around her neck and there was very little amniotic fluid. I was asked to return to hospital the next day to be induced. This time, from the moment I arrived I was never without a midwife, and often a doctor attended too. I began to feel that something was wrong, and eventually they admitted that the baby was showing signs of being distressed. A couple of hours later, the decision had been taken to perform a Caesarean section, and after signing the relevant papers I was whisked to theatre and given a general anaesthetic.

Baby Hannah came into the world weighing just over 6 lb and was handed to Ken, after the necessary checks had been performed. When I came round, I gazed lovingly at this long and scrawny mite, her skin white and scaly due to the fluids having dried up. Though very thankful to God for a second child, I told myself this was it. No more!

Our new diocese was Lichfield, in the West Midlands. Ken was to be the curate at St Peter's Collegiate Church in the centre of Wolverhampton, and soon after we'd settled in I got in touch with the DDO's office. Mark Geldard immediately incorporated me into their process and within months it had been confirmed that I was to be put through to a Bishop's Advisory Panel (BAP). Travelling up to Manchester for the interview that was to decide my future direction was terrifying. All the years of believing God had called me and would continue to nurture this call were about to be put to the test. If it was a 'no', I could still continue as an evangelist with the Church Army, but I very much hoped for a positive response. Feeling naked and exposed, I wrapped myself in prayer.

The day came and I and my fellow candidates were introduced to our assessors: an all-white panel of middle-class individuals with little, or insufficient, knowledge of my cultural background. If I am honest, I did wonder how I would be received in this setting. Repeating the Serenity Prayer as a mantra, I reminded myself it was all about accepting what I had no control over, acting on what I could, and – most importantly – seeking wisdom to differentiate between the two.

I answered question after question, I performed the two exercises we were given to do, I ate in the communal dining room, I entered fully into the worship, and a few days later the news came in.

I had been accepted!

It was a vindication of years of waiting and hoping.

My family situation meant my training was to be part-time on the West Midlands Ministerial Training Course at Queen's Foundation in Birmingham – an ecumenical training environment where I'd meet individuals from other denominational backgrounds. We were lucky that our leaders included the Revd John Wilkinson and the Revd Andrew Wingate, who were genuinely committed to ecumenism and believed passionately that theology should have cultural relevance. We gained so much from being at Queen's during their time. These two men allowed us to think deeply and broadly, and to root our understanding in God's generosity.

I remember listening to a lecture by the Revd Canon Dr Alison Joyce, and realising the Old Testament was not only coming alive for me, but powerfully connecting with the person I now was. For example, I could now see the book of Esther through the lens of modern relevance. Esther tells the story of two women in a man's world. First, there is Queen Vashti, who refuses to appear and dance in public before the king because he is clearly drunk and, evidently, not great at handling challenging situations on the home front. His friends suggest that if it becomes known the queen does not obey her husband, chaos will ensue: 'This very day the noble ladies of Persia and Media who have heard of the queen's behaviour will rebel against the king's officials, and there will be no end of contempt and wrath!' (Esther 1:18). The king gives in to this ridiculous argument and gets rid of the queen. His search for her successor results in Esther, who has found favour in his eyes, taking her place. When trouble arises, Esther is asked to advocate on behalf of the people; she tries to excuse herself and has to be reminded that she is in her current role 'for just such a time as this' (Esther 4:14).

Equally powerful was the teaching we were offered on contextual and black theology, which sought to liberate those of African descent from a sense of oppression. Whatever differences there may be in terms of ethnicity, culture, class and economic health, we are one people. I was recognising for the first time that Afrocentric and Liberation theologies are just as valuable as Eurocentric ones, and this meant that people who looked like me had something to say.

I remember a sense of freedom washing over me. I was allowed to think and feel without constraint. I no longer had to try to slot myself into a preconceived notion of faith. Not only was I allowed to choose, but I was getting all the tools I needed to walk my path, and to help others find theirs.

The Spirit of God was flowing freely.

I am for ever indebted to the experience I gained at Queen's, as it allowed me to draw closer to a great big God who did not need to be protected or defended. As I watch certain sections of the Church building impregnable walls, I cannot help but think that their God must be very small.

10
JUGGLING MOTHERHOOD AND MINISTRY

BEING ACCEPTED FOR TRAINING into the ordained ministry meant that the call I had received as a teenager was truly becoming a reality. On a more prosaic level, 'reality' meant Ken and I constantly juggling our diaries: we had to make the impossible possible when it came to managing ministerial work, studies and family. Lectures for me were mainly on a midweek evening, and there were a certain number of weekend commitments each term too.

One Saturday, I was at Queen's when I received a message that something had happened, but the children were now OK. I was puzzled, yet quickly put the matter out of my mind. Ken hadn't gone into detail, so the incident must have been a minor one. Perhaps they had spilled the milk or knocked over a jar of jam – Ken knew I was not good with unnecessary messy situations, so he was possibly giving me advance notice! Though I checked in again later and tried to prompt him, he wouldn't say more. In retrospect, that should have flagged something for me, but he was full of reassurance that there was no need to worry, so I didn't.

When I got home that evening, Ken was doing the dishes. He hardly glanced up as I came into the kitchen.

'The children are upstairs waiting for you.'

I dropped my bags where I stood and rushed up to the girls' bedroom. As soon as she saw me, Amanda burst out,

'Mommy, Mommy, Hannah fell into the ducks' water and Daddy fished her out.' Seeing the look of shock on my face, she immediately added, 'Mommy, don't be angry with him, don't be angry.'

I looked up to see Ken framed in the doorway. 'Darling, where were you?' I asked.

His response was, 'I was sitting in the pushchair!'

To this day, I remain unable to be angry with him about it. How could I after our two-year-old's plea? But later that night Ken and I reflected on the tragedy that could have been. Within days, there were other similar incidents reported in the news of children falling into a duck pond in their local park. Sadly, all of these ended in heartbreak. It made us realise just how close we came to losing one of our daughters, and I truly felt the bereaved parents' pain.

A wise old priest once said to me, 'Rose, God does not call you to something like family and then years down the line call you to something else that destroys the first call.'

I have held on to this throughout my ministry, regularly checking in to make sure I'm carrying out the various roles I inhabit well. Sometimes, though, I can get so absorbed in what I'm doing that I forget to care for myself, even in the simple things ...

One Saturday afternoon, engrossed in a session at college, I delayed far too long before going for a comfort break. The men's facility was on the ground floor, the ladies' above on the first floor. I knew I would not make it upstairs, so as I pushed open the door of the men's, I shouted, 'There is a woman coming in, but don't worry, I'm married so I've seen it all before.'

To my surprise, a voice boomed out, 'You haven't seen this one.'

I was not deterred, I'm afraid – I just made sure to avert my gaze. I was desperate and I was going to go!

The arguments surrounding the admission of women to the priesthood were still raging while I was at Queen's, and it was challenging preparing for ordination against the backdrop of what felt like a 'hostile environment'. At this point, it was only admissible for women to be ordained as deacons. If women could not be priests, then we were fast becoming, by default, permanent deacons in the Church of England. The key role of the diaconate was centred around serving – to attend to the sick and the poor, those on the edge of society and often seen as outcast. In the absence of a priest, deacons could preach, baptise and help in 'instructing others in the catechism'; they could assist the priest with the distribution of Holy Communion and the reading of Scripture too. But unlike priests, they were not permitted to preside at communion, hear confessions or anoint the sick. Deep down I believed I was being called to exercise a priestly ministry. Nonetheless, for the time being, a temporary line had been drawn, restricting what I could and could not do, and I would have to live with this. I was prepared to wait. My calling was of God. He would make it happen.

There were those who claimed the Church was failing to follow Scripture; that it was being influenced by feminism and – horror of horrors – talk of equality. Some conservative evangelical Christians expressed their displeasure in a way that appeared reminiscent of a fairly repressive worldview. Apparently, as women, we should be at home and obeying the instructions of our husbands, brothers and fathers, simply because they were men! Those from the Anglo-Catholic tradition were equally confident that as Jesus was male, it must mean that we should precisely follow that male line of tradition. Worse still was the argument that since the Roman Catholics had not led the way on this, we Anglicans couldn't possibly presume to take the lead ourselves! I do remember thinking: *If your understanding is that the essence of true religion lies with the Roman Catholic Church – even though it does not recognise your own ordination – why don't you go over to Rome?*

What fills me with despair, even today, is the fact that there are intelligent women who share some of these views! Bob Marley's 'Redemption Song' expresses my thoughts far better than I ever could: we are asked to free ourselves from the things that oppress us and weigh us down, and remember that we have a choice. I truly believe that, as women, we continue to suffer from internalised oppression. I, for one, do not want my daughters to grow up believing that because of their gender they are limited in terms of their vocation or any other life choice.

Back in the late 1980s, every time it looked as though there could be a breakthrough, with the numbers beginning to stack up sufficiently for the vote for women priests to get through General Synod, we'd be inundated with threats of people walking away from the Church. It felt as though the hierarchy, fearing an impending schism and wanting to do everything possible to hold the Church together, was repeatedly rowing back. (Not that anything would pacify those who did not wish to see women ordained to the priesthood.) I interpreted this to mean, 'As women you can cope, so we can afford to let you down.'

People were agonising at all levels. You could hear them at odds with one another throughout parishes, deaneries and dioceses. Everyone wanted to have their say, and different ecumenical arguments were constantly being put forward on both sides of the debate. I remember once asking, in response to the argument that this would ruin our relationship with the Roman Catholics and the Orthodox, 'Do we not care about our relationship with the Methodists, who already have women in ministry?'

It became clear that there were members of Parliament's Ecclesiastical Committee who were demanding a compromise package before they would give their support. Everyone knew that those for or those against would need a two-thirds majority in all three Houses (bishops, elected clergy and elected laity) of the General Synod. The aforementioned committee would then need to give the 'all clear' before any decision could be implemented.

Women being rejected by the Church has given me some dark moments. I have wrestled with feeling complicit in this. I am, after all, part of a church that does not embrace the ministry of women with joy.

However, despite the unease with which some continued to regard women being included in holy orders (the sacrament through which bishops, priests and deacons receive the power and grace to perform their sacred duties), I'm pleased to report that my service of ordination to the diaconate in 1991 passed uneventfully. I am thankful to God that there was much joy among those who had come to celebrate with me, including Faye, my adopted mom, and Calvin McIntyre, a long-time friend who was serving as a priest in the USA. The cathedral was packed, as was usual for ordinations, and our diocesan bishop, the Right Revd Keith Sutton, graciously took care to ensure the service was a very special experience for us. As women, we were aware that the male deacons in our cohort would seamlessly become ordained priests the following year. Not so us. Our destiny was to continue as deacons.

A few weeks after my ordination, I was giving the girls a bath when I was called away for a few moments. I came back to find them arguing.

'OK, OK. What's going on?'

They were at odds with each other about who between them should be Mommy and who should be Daddy.

'Why do you want to be Mommy?' I asked.

Amanda piped up, 'Daddies go to work and mommies go to London!'

Clearly they'd taken note of the fact that I was regularly jumping on the train south to attend a variety of meetings. Another time in the car when they were arguing, it was about Mommy being a leader in the Church! Wow, I thought, the children had noticed something different and, here they were, both wanting to be me.

I began my ordained ministry at the conservative evangelical church of St Matthew's, Wolverhampton, where the PCC held the view that women should not have authority over men. This meant they struggled somewhat with the idea of having a female curate. I am told that at one stage in the discussion with the vicar, they even asked if it was possible to have Ken instead of me! Despite the turbulence behind the scenes, however, I felt a strong conviction that St Matthew's was the right place to be.

The Revd Jim McManus and his wife Mavis were a very gentle yet resolute couple. Jim was keen to appoint me and I had said yes, so he was not backing down. I wondered if the PCC's disquiet had anything to do with the colour of my skin, but I never got a direct reply. I did learn later that its members had resigned en bloc, but my 'yes' was still strong and I knew this was the Spirit at work. Some of the congregation had welcomed me warmly and I could see that there were good people among them, even if they held views from the Middle Ages about women.

Nonetheless, the human being within me was unable to dismiss the fact that a powerful element did not want me. I had to spend time in prayer, and one result of this was that I decided, right from the start, not to use my position to 'preach' about, or indeed try to prove, why God was calling women to serve in the Church. I was there for the sake of the gospel and nothing else. The words of the well-known hymn provided me with some solace:

Just as I am, without one plea,
but that thy blood was shed for me,
and that thou bidd'st me come to thee,
O Lamb of God, I come, I come.
Charlotte Elliott (1836)

Deep down, I knew this curacy had the potential to fail. However, for me failure was not an option. This meant I was driven in a way that few of my fellow ordinands were likely to be, and the words of the prayer authored by St Ignatius became a daily mantra:

Teach us, good Lord,
to serve you as you deserve,
to give and not to count the cost,
to fight and not to heed the wounds,
to toil and not to seek for rest,
to labour and not to ask for any rewards,
save that of knowing that we do your will.
St Ignatius of Loyola

Some weeks after my arrival, I had to have keyhole surgery on my knee. Realistically, I needed some time off work to recuperate. But my thinking went something like this: *You need to get back to work. You can't have them saying, 'See, I told you – she's a woman'; or, 'She's black; she can't hack it.'* As a result, I got Ken to drive me over to the parish and hobbled around with walking sticks!

The sad thing is that if I had to do this all over again today, I don't know, hand on heart, if I'd do anything differently. This is a matter of regret. I'm conscious of carrying the weight of the knowledge that I am a woman, and a black woman; I don't have the option of being second best or mediocre, because other black women need to come after me, and how I perform will determine how they are received.

I often ponder that when recruits are being selected for a post previously inhabited by a white man, no one says, 'We've had one of those before – we won't do that again!' It's definitely a different story when it comes to women and visible minorities.

I felt the hand of God guiding me through my curacy. Prayer was my song, and the joy of the Lord was indeed my

1 Baby Rose with mother and sisters 2 Father Joe
3 Shirley and Rose with Aunt Pet

4 With fiancé Ken   5 Wedding day with adopted mom and daddy
6 With both sets of parents

7 The day of Rose's priesting   8 With Shirley after first service as priest
9 En route to a party

10 The day legistlation for women priests was approved
11 Hannah, Jamie and Amanda
12 'The vicar on the roof' and curate Richenda
13 With Archbishop Desmond Tutu

14 Skydiving to raise funds   15 Twenty-fifth wedding anniversary
16 Hannah and David's wedding in Jamaica
17 With mother and grandchild Arthur

18 With President Barack Obama in Central Lobby, Palace of Westminster
© House of Commons
19 Tributes paid to murdered Labour MP Jo Cox © Matt Cardy/gettyimages

20

21

22

20 Consecration at St Paul's Cathedral
21 Outside St Paul's with Jermain Jackman
22 Rose's official invitation to the Coronation of King Charles III and Queen Camilla

23

24

23 With Queen Camilla, Kanya King & Marie Hanson © WPA Pool/gettyimages
24 In conversation with King Charles

strength. I was living my diaconal role, always glad to be with people just where they were, taking time to pray with them, and often weeping with them too when they lost loved ones. At the crematorium, I would often hear comments on how wonderful the service had been and, on more than one occasion, 'If my vicar looked like/preached like that, I would go to church.' The wider community I was reaching out to was responding, slowly but surely.

At home, of course, I was Mother to Amanda and Hannah, and I discovered quite early on how important it was to find a pattern that enabled me to fulfil my ministry while assuming the main childcare role. Spending my day off cleaning the house from top to bottom and being exhausted by evening simply could not continue!

So I devised the following. My preferred time for prayer was as soon as I got up, but I now decided to have breakfast with the children and drop them at nursery and school before going into work mode, beginning with my morning prayers. I would then spend some hours engaging with parish duties before collecting them at 3 p.m. The rest of the afternoon was devoted to listening to their day, taking them dancing, preparing our evening meal and getting them ready for bed. Cooking in bulk and freezing in appropriate dinner-size portions helped on busy days too.

If I had a funeral in the afternoon, I would ask the parents of one of their friends to meet them from school and keep them until Ken or I could collect them. If I needed to make an afternoon visit, I'd sometimes just take them along with me.

Evening meetings could often be held at home. If I had to attend an event elsewhere or make an urgent visit, Ken might be available to look after the girls. I was once very cross when I overheard him telling a caller on the phone that he could not do something as he was babysitting his children. 'You are their father,' I shouted, 'not a babysitter!'

I can't recall ever failing to attend to something connected with my ministry by using the girls as an excuse for not being there. The new pattern I devised meant that although I did not have a day off as such, there were three hours every weekday afternoon to fill as need be.

I was running a tight ship. I had to. I was a parent of young children. This routine worked for me.

11
THE JOURNEY TO PRIESTHOOD

WITHIN A YEAR OF BEGINNING my curacy, Jim McManus became unwell. It was discovered that he needed back surgery, and he was on sick leave for several months before eventually retiring due to ill health. I was now without a training incumbent, and although it is the church-wardens' responsibility to run things during a vacancy, it probably won't come as a surprise that, while working closely alongside the wardens, I did not hesitate to embrace the opportunity to show leadership. I ended up being the de facto go-to person – exactly the kind of situation that those prominent lay leadership objectors had feared. The very idea of a woman in charge!

Fortunately, they soon realised that my interest was not in power but in attending to God's mission. I had no doubt that steering the church in that direction was the right thing to do. Drawing on my Church Army training, and depending greatly on the grace of God, I sought to gather people together in fellowship to pray, to study the Scriptures together, to grow in faith and to be outward-facing in the community. Long after I left, members were still talking about that time as a truly momentous period.

Yet though there were blessings, there were also challenges. One was making the worship times work for all the church family. The main service was at 9:30 a.m. and families who attended did not stay on for the Sunday school at 11 a.m. Of the three or four Sunday school teachers we had, only one regularly attended the early 9:30 a.m. service. I held a series of consultations and proposed changing the time of Sunday worship to 10:30 a.m. This was a big deal. We decided to go with it for ten months before sharing frankly how we felt things were working out. The response when the time was up turned out to be almost wholly positive, and I will always look back on this initiative with a great sense of achievement. Now families were coming to services together, the children were participating in Sunday school, and their teachers were becoming part of the worshipping life of the church.

I faced other testing times too. One afternoon, I had a call from a church member to say she'd been reading about the death of the wife of an elderly church member in the local paper. I was surprised not to have been informed of the bereavement earlier, because this was a couple I'd been visiting regularly; indeed, I'd been taking them home communion every month. As long-term members of the church, they had at various times taken on the role of churchwarden, served on committees and taught in the Sunday school. The husband had remained in the family home when his wife's deteriorating health meant she had to go into a care home. I had taken him to visit her there on her birthday, so they could be together, and it was very moving to observe the love they had for each other after more than fifty years of marriage. I had felt close to them, and now I longed to support him, knowing what this loss would mean.

Gathering up my two girls, we went to pay him a visit. He confirmed that his wife had passed.

'Why didn't you let me know?' I asked. 'And why is the service not being held in the church where you both served for a lifetime?'

His reply was surprising: 'My children said the funeral directors told them that as we are no longer living in the parish, it can't be there, so you cannot officiate at the service.'

This did not quite ring true. As they were on the electoral roll of St Matthew's, there had to be something else. Sensing his grief, I resisted asking further questions, simply repeating my condolences and praying with him before leaving. I felt rather unsettled.

The next morning, after dropping the children off, I drove to the funeral directors and asked to see the person who was dealing with the family. I wanted to know why they felt I couldn't officiate at the service.

The funeral director shifted uncomfortably before blurting out: 'Well, the family told us that their father did not want you to do the service.'

How could this be possible? We were talking about a dear soul who had warmly welcomed me each month, and whom I had taken on a number of occasions to visit his wife in her care home.

Suddenly, the agenda became clear. This had nothing to do with the father's wishes, and everything to do with those of the family. The funeral was to be held at the crematorium and a priest from the deanery (who was opposed to women in holy orders) was asked to officiate. Services at the crematorium are each given a slot of twenty minutes. On the day, the service lasted ten minutes – ten minutes to celebrate the life of someone who had contributed so much to the Church during her lifetime.

After the service I handed the family a letter in which I offered my condolences, listed my involvement with their parents and shared how sad I was to have been prevented from serving their mother in death. Unbeknown to me, the family complained to my bishop, who, instead of contacting me to ask for my side of the story or indeed for an explanation, sent me a message asking me to cease and desist from visiting the father. I promptly sent him a message back: 'When you tell me what to say to the father as to why I can no longer visit him, then I will consider stopping. Until then I will continue to care for him pastorally.' And I did!

But though I kept visiting and taking him home communion, I was careful never to give any hint of what had unfolded. When he died, the same priest who had taken his wife's funeral was asked to officiate a second time. Once again, the service was over in ten minutes. I attended but did not seek to engage with the family. As far as I was concerned, I had made my point and there was no need to repeat it.

Back in 1975, the General Synod had agreed that there was no fundamental theological basis for prohibiting women from being priests or bishops. Yet here we were in 1992, the second year of my curacy, and the General Synod and its various committees hadn't made much progress at all. As one of the 1,400 or so women ordained to the diaconate and waiting to be ordained priest, I fielded many media interviews and took part in a few news panels too. I struggled inwardly sometimes, especially when I was sharing TV studios with women who were saying no to other women. Numerous newspaper articles weighed up the pros and cons. Deep down, I prayed that the Church would allow itself to be guided by the Holy Spirit through those who would be voting; the danger was that 'party groups' – comprising evangelicals, Anglo-Catholics or liberals – were encouraging their members to vote together in a particular way.

When the time came for the vote in Synod, on Remembrance Day 1992, hundreds of us gathered in Dean's Yard. Church House stood to our south, the offices of Westminster Abbey to our north, and the Choir School east and west. We were singing and praying and there was a great buzz all around us.

And then Synod voted … in favour!

The disparity in response was marked.

In the chambers of Church House, those present were asked to receive the vote in silence. It was almost as if the people in favour were the 'mistress' everyone knew about but didn't want to speak of in public, in case the 'real wife' (the people who considered themselves to be protecting the orthodox faith) should become upset. Those in the gallery also had to receive the vote in silence.

For those of us congregated in Dean's Yard, however, there were no such restrictions. We were able to release our joy and expressed this fittingly in the words of the song used as the theme for Barack Obama's presidency: 'It's been a long time coming.' But there were tears too, because we knew first-hand the pain that had accompanied this journey for many in the Church, some of whom would now be deemed too old to start the process.

And it was disquieting that although the vote had attained the required two-thirds majority, it seemed to have been passed grudgingly. In fact, it would not have gone through at all if it hadn't been for the behind-the-scenes negotiation that 'flying bishops' should be introduced. This, in effect, created a two-tier system, which meant that those who did not wish to be associated with the Church's decision to ordain women could ask for alternative or extended episcopal oversight. This same Church which had taught us that the grace associated with the Eucharist is dependent on God, not the officiating priest, seemed to be having trouble sticking to this line if the officiating priest was to be a woman!

Bishops who had ordained women as priests were, in effect, themselves 'blacklisted', no longer deemed acceptable to conduct ordinations for those not in favour of women's ordination. Some diocesan bishops decided they would only ordain deacons in their dioceses. This would mean they would always be acceptable to those against women's priestly ordination. I often wondered if these diocesan bishops realised what message they were sending. Far from signifying that they remained neutral, they were making a clear choice, and it meant that concerns regarding the implication for female priests appeared not to be in the frame much at all. But then we were women; we could cope!

Looking back, I cannot help but believe that, under the guise of unity, we made a grave error of judgement, setting a precedence that allows anyone (usually those identifying as 'orthodox', whatever wing of the Church they belong to) to create their own line of episcopacy if they do not agree with properly taken synodical decisions. In effect, instead of achieving something positive, we actually legitimised discrimination against women. By trying to make sure that certain voices or camps were listened to, I believe we pushed the gospel imperative to second place. I still wonder if where we have settled today can possibly be regarded as 'real' unity.

In the end, women are still the ones being excluded and left to feel that they are somehow second best. In response to 'orthodox' thinking, they are repeatedly called upon to make sacrifices; to graciously step back so that their male colleagues can be affirmed in their maleness and rightness to inhabit the space of priesthood. And yet the flying-bishop system we embraced and adopted promised we would all be flourishing! There are times when I feel like the mother of the baby in the Judgement of Solomon. You'll recall that in response to two mothers, one whose baby was alive and the other with a dead baby, who each claimed the living one as their own, Solomon offered to halve the living infant. The real mother's immediate response was to say, 'Let her keep the baby,' so he wouldn't come to harm. There is a part of me that feels deeply it would have been better to wait until the Church was ready to accept women wholeheartedly than for us to be the kind of segregated Church we are now, pretending to be one.

Following the vote, the race was on to be the first diocese to ordain women to the priesthood. Bishop Barry Rogerson knew there was no reason to wait, and a date was announced for the first thirty-two women to be ordained as Church of England priests in Bristol Cathedral. A journalist from my local newspaper, the Wolverhampton *Express & Star*, had tickets to the service on 12 March 1994 and, wanting to record my immediate reaction, invited me to attend. The expectation leading up to the event was great.

Having made sure Hannah had had a great birthday party with her friends the day before, courtesy of McDonald's so there was no tidying up for me to do afterwards, the journalist and I headed to Bristol with great expectations, probably for different reasons. The service was surreal. Space was given to protesters to object in 'a respectful and orderly way' – a very British way of going about things. Only then would the ordination service progress.

My sense was that in allowing for this 'orderly' protest – which occurred at several ordination services up and down the country as the year progressed – the Church was essentially being complicit in ensuring that there remained a permanent question mark over the legitimacy of women in holy orders.

In my head I know that I am legitimately ordained, but real-life experiences of women on the ground being 'legitimately' rejected make it difficult to believe this is truly so. I understand that *The Five Guiding Principles: Guidance for Candidates for Ordination in the Church of England* was created by the Church in order to help make the ordination of women more acceptable, by acknowledging that others hold legitimate theological views to the contrary, but can we really have it both ways? Despite these 'Principles', it is again women who are left to bear the scars of the Church's attempt to hold two views simultaneously. My heart longs for a Church that can move forward with honesty and integrity; that is willing to say, 'Right now we do not believe exactly the same things, but we will walk side by side and work hand in hand for the sake of the gospel of Jesus Christ.'

But then, for a while, other matters had to take precedence. On my return from Bristol I began packing for an urgent trip to Jamaica.

News had come through that Joe, my birth father, had died.

12

CLOSING ONE DOOR AND OPENING ANOTHER

JOE HAD BEEN ILL FOR SOME TIME, and Shirley and I had already made a number of visits to see him. This man who had never been there for us, emotionally or financially, now needed our provision – as Christians, we had no doubt of that. At one stage, Ken and I seriously considered the possibility of the girls and I temporarily setting up home with him in Jamaica. Fortunately, that proved unnecessary, as Shirley and I managed to put in place appropriate support structures and arrange daily care.

The flight to Jamaica felt longer than usual. Joe's death was bringing back many memories from childhood and most of them were negative. The one that distressed me most concerned his response when I requested money to buy ingredients for my fourth-form home economics class. Unimpressed that I had been sent to him for financial assistance, he bellowed, 'Goh ask di Prime Minister fi money!' I walked away feeling humiliated, though deep down I'd had little doubt what the outcome would be. Joe blamed the government for the high cost of living and hence his poverty. He had never given me anything more than small change for ice cream, but as a child sent on an errand, I had no other choice but to 'beg' for money from a father who had no idea of the responsibilities that came with his role. I've already spoken of the frustration throughout my growing-up years of having a parent who, even when he was present, refused to engage with us, his children.

Shirley, who had migrated to the USA, flew down to join me from her home in California. Together we arranged for the funeral service to be held at St Francis Mission in Glendevon, the little mission church we'd grown up in. That seemed fitting, as one of our happier memories of Joe was of him bringing sugar cane, avocados, breadfruit and bananas, all grown in his yard, to the church every Harvest Thanksgiving. Now he would return to the building a final time for his last rites.

The rector, the Revd Justin Nembhard, officiated at the service; Shirley read the eulogy she had written, having consulted with the family, and we played Ray Charles's cover version of the Beatles' 'Yesterday'. The second verse of that song, about not being half the man I used to be, continues to tug at my heart strings whenever I think of my father.

As I preached, I shared the story of the time Joe turned up at my primary school dressed in stained, torn clothes, with a box on his head and a machete in his hand. Having spotted him in the distance, I promptly hurried away from the school gate to hide behind one of the buildings, but unfortunately he'd seen me.

His voice boomed out, 'Rose, a whey you a run fram mi fah?'

I had no alternative but to return to where he was, by the gate in the school yard. By now a group of children playing nearby had gathered to see what was unfolding. 'A yuh fada?' (Is this your father?) they asked.

I remember being most embarrassed, having to acknowledge this was indeed the case. When I got home that evening, I told Aunt Pet about the encounter and remember her being quite sympathetic.

Carrying on with my sermon, I explained how I had come to connect this story with the poem 'Song of the Banana Man'. I then recited the piece, in which the central figure is a man seen in the marketplace wearing stained, torn clothing. He is mistaken for a beggar but speaks of his pride at being a banana man, even though he may be looking rather scruffy. In many ways my father was a proud soul. His yard was like a repair shop, but he lacked the financial resources to make it a real success. He would collect lots of old stuff that people had thrown away and, in his own time, make things that he would eventually sell. He would also use his wheelbarrow to carry stones to the many places in the local community where there were potholes, and pack these stones in to fill them up.

I still find myself asking, 'Who was this man?' The obstacles that prevented him journeying to emotional, psychological and spiritual maturity – political upheaval in Cuba, migration to Jamaica, his mother's mental ill-health and the lack of a father figure – were truly substantial. The reality is that Joe represents many men in my country of birth who are simply a shadow of all that God created them to be. Instead of engaging with the work we all need to do to develop, they stunt themselves by hiding behind cultural norms and practices, sometimes invoking the name of slavery and the legacy of brokenness. It has occurred to me that this may offer some kind of insight into those who stand against women being ordained: perhaps a combination of fear and stubbornness prevents them from seeing and experiencing the new things that God is doing among them.

I still think about the father I never had. Nonetheless, I am thankful for those moments when he did, in his own way, show signs of being proud of Shirley and me; when he boasted to those in his local community, 'A fi mi daughta dem' (Those are my daughters), perhaps he was trying to say that he had got one thing right. That he had done something worthwhile.

I made a conscious decision to keep his name. I guess the little girl who ran from him at the school gate all those years ago now wanted to say, 'Joseph Hudson was my father.'

I would be ordained priest as Rose *Hudson*-Wilkin.

The morning after the funeral, I passed a travel agent that was advertising day-trips to Havana, Cuba. I walked in and booked right there and then! That short visit took me to places I could imagine my father and his siblings would have known as young children, and the whole day proved a truly cathartic experience.

Returning to Montego Bay, I set about packing and saying farewell to friends and family, managing to spend some quality time with my adopted mom and dad before heading for the airport. As the flight was taxiing on the runway, the man in the seat next to me asked about my visit. He was a tourist and had had a wonderful time. My response was to burst into uncontrollable tears, and it was some time before I could answer his question! He was very apologetic, but I assured him that he was not to blame for my distress. I needed to cry a lifetime of tears for the father I had never really had. It dawned on me later that this was the first time I'd wept for him since his death.

Back in England, it was a rush to catch up on all I'd missed over the last fortnight and to clear my desk before I needed to go off on retreat. When I returned after two and a half weeks, I would be priested.

The Sunday before I left, one of the female members of the church came up to me with tears in her eyes. She hesitated before saying, 'I was one of those who resigned from the PCC when you came to us. I want you to know that I've changed my mind and I do believe that God has called you and that he calls women.'

I hugged her and thanked her for her affirmation. I'm glad to say that since my departure from that parish, other female curates have been appointed, and the church has also put forward women from the congregation for ordination!

As 23 April 1994 dawned, the joy all around was palpable. It was very special that Shirley had come across from California to join other family and friends for my big day. The BBC in the Midlands ran a special piece on the ordination of women, and my new training incumbent, though initially reluctant, agreed to them filming the service and later interviewing me and others who attended. We made the local news for the region! The happy, relaxed reception that followed centred around the wonderful celebratory cake made by my neighbour and friend Jo Clothier.

Twenty-two years after receiving God's call to the ordained ministry at the age of fourteen, my priesting marked the beginning of a thrilling new chapter. God had journeyed with me through the darkness of rejection. He had carried me when I needed to be carried, and I could rest assured that he would stay by my side.

Deeply grateful, I recommitted my life and ministry to him.

13
GROWING (BOTH) FAMILIES

THE GIRLS WERE BEGINNING TO ASK if they could have a baby brother. Ken and I were open to the idea, my thoughts being (and I was only half joking), *I am not going through the pain of childbirth again. Let's adopt instead.* Ken, having watched me give birth twice (though he did have to step outside for the emergency Caesarean), was happy to agree that we had been there, done that and got the T-shirt. It would be good for us to begin exploring the possibility of adopting a little boy in response to the children's request. And so, thanks to an organisation called Barnardo's, Jamie joined our family approximately three months before his fourth birthday.

He was an energetic child who'd been given up for adoption at birth. Sadly, due to his caseworker's heavy workload, he'd been left in foster care, albeit with a wonderful foster mother who loved him dearly. I vividly recall her tears on the day we went to collect him and bring him home; both of them were utterly inconsolable, and it felt as if we were stealing him away from the family he had known since birth.

Ken drove while I sat in the back of the car with Jamie. I often ponder whether my own tears on the day came from knowing what it feels like to be taken from a place and a community; to be abruptly transported from the known to the unknown. We had willingly chosen to extend our family;

Jamie had had no choice but to become part of it. It is good to remember that we walk the path of faith as followers as well as leaders. Today, knowing the journey he's been on, I watch Jamie with some pride as he continues to unfold into a loving son and a sensitive and attentive father. He is still a work in progress.

Amanda and Hannah were excited to meet their little brother, and I had taken maternity leave so I could be at home for his first three months and help him settle in. Whenever he asked after his foster mom, I would phone her so they could speak to each other. We were given albums with photos relating to his family story and would spend time looking at these, talking about the different people in the pictures. His father's mother was Jamaican. Perhaps that tipped the scales in terms of the foster mom he had had and the agreement that he should come to be part of a dual-heritage family. He was already well versed in the school of reggae and Bob Marley, and was very black in his mannerisms.

Despite being bright, however, our son struggled to stay within the boundaries of acceptable behaviour. This led to many a challenging meeting at school and to confrontations both there and at home. Other friends who had adopted were experiencing similar ups and downs, and I remember thinking at the time that these were probably just par for the course. The challenges continued during the rest of our time in the Midlands, throughout Jamie's primary schooling and the start of his secondary education when we moved to London. He did have some good teachers, but I didn't always feel supported by the school system, or that we were all singing from the same hymn sheet when it came to following through.

As a family, we engaged with whatever counselling support we could find, and although we soon came to the realisation that there was no 'right' way to cope when things got particularly testing, we did grow a little in wisdom and understanding. The truth was that Jamie appeared lost, always insisting on having his own way, only doing what he wanted and refusing to follow anyone else's instructions. When he said he was interested in football, I gently pointed out that the game was not just about kicking a ball around; if he was on the pitch, he would need to do what he was told in order to remain there! We did notice that he related well to the older Caribbean ladies in the congregation, to whom he was always polite; perhaps they reminded him of his foster mother.

Alongside these recurring family dramas, I was navigating ministerial life. Quite frankly, without the grace of God I would simply have crumbled under the pressure.

When my curacy in Wolverhampton ended, I moved to West Bromwich, taking up two part-time roles. One was Associate Priest at the Church of the Good Shepherd; the second, wholly new for the diocese, was Diocesan Officer for Black Anglican Concerns. This post had been created in response to various national debates surrounding racism, in which questions were being asked about the lack of black people and other minorities in leadership within the Church. Successive surveys carried out by the Committee for Minority Ethnic Anglican Concerns had revealed that there were significant numbers of people from such backgrounds worshipping in the Church of England. However, although they were in our pews, they were not to be seen in any significant roles, such as PCC membership, churchwarden, deacon, priest or bishop.

Contrary to talk of the Church organising a 'Black Caucus' (this was so far from the truth), I saw my first task as creating awareness around the issues involved. As ever, I was also determined to challenge the status quo, by helping to equip people for ordained and lay ministry and introducing minority ethnic people from across the diocese to one another. I felt very strongly that to make a real success of my work, I would need to speak not only to black audiences, but to predominantly white audiences too.

One such, in rural Staffordshire, was comprised of church-wardens. On an Archdeacon's Visitation I asked them: 'If you had a vacancy here and I applied for it, would you consider me?'

One warden popped her hand up, so I invited her to speak. And speak she did! 'We have no black people here, so why would we consider you?'

Despite being shocked to the core by her response, I was quick to reply, and I did so with a smile. 'Oh, so white people can go to Africa, Asia and the Caribbean; white people can work in our inner cities in predominantly black churches; but black priests can only work with black people? How very interesting.'

She had brought home one uncomfortable truth with a resounding thud. If we fail to be honest about the fact that, left to our own devices, we simply choose the people who look like us and speak like us, nothing will ever change. But the tragedy of not pushing beyond our comfort zones is that our gloriously diverse family under God never realises its full potential.

John writes in 1 John 4:20, 'Those who say, "I love God", and hate their brothers or sisters, are liars; for those who do not love a brother or sister whom they have seen, cannot love God whom they have not seen.' This gospel imperative demands that we don't merely speak words of inclusivity but show through our actions that we truly love our 'sisters and brothers'. It won't happen all at once, but we can certainly work towards having a just world and a just Church where no differentiation is possible. By acknowledging that we belong, notwithstanding our creed or colour or name, we can be both followers and leaders – followers of the gospel and our conscience, and leaders of others. Little children, in their own rainbow colours, will be able to see reflections of themselves in all walks of life; they will grow up knowing that they can become whatever they believe they are called to be, in the world and in the Church.

Unsurprisingly, I experienced a certain amount of resistance from a variety of different quarters. There were those who said, 'We don't have any black people here, so we don't have a problem,' and it was interesting to note that some of the strongest and most negative views about black people were expressed by people in very rural places where there were either few or no black people at all.

The term 'political correctness' was becoming more prevalent, and I witnessed frequent instances of it being weaponised against the Church and other organisations when they tried to address the lack of black people in leadership roles. On several occasions, having been accused of seeking to be politically correct, I counter-argued that we, as a Church, could not speak prophetically to the world on this subject if we did not address it in our own backyard.

While absorbed in this piece of work, I was aware of three things disturbing my spirit. First, whenever I addressed the need for more black people in leadership, some commentator would pop up with: 'But we need qualified people,' implying that black people were unlikely to have the necessary ability or education.

Visiting within the Diocese of Lichfield where Wedgwood china is made, I was informed with breathtaking frankness, 'We don't have any black people here, because we need skilled people.'

When I did not rise to this remark, it was repeated, and I couldn't help myself! I responded to the gentleman with a question of my own: 'Were you born with the ability to make Wedgwood, or were you trained?'

'We are trained,' he replied.

To which I responded, 'Well, black people are capable of being trained too, you know!'

The second thing that disturbed me, and still does, was talk of 'positive discrimination'. I hear myself screaming inside, *No, not positive discrimination. Discrimination is discrimination!* Then I tell myself, *Calm down, Rose! Breathe!* For me, it's not about positive discrimination but rather positive action. For example, when two people are interviewed for a job, and on paper there seems to be no difference between them – their references are equally good and both interview well – then taking positive action would mean the interviewer, on behalf of their organisation, looking at the staff already employed and making a positive choice around building a diverse workforce in terms of ethnic background and, of course, gender too. This kind of constructive action becomes self-fulfilling and therefore unnecessary in the long run, as making fair choices ensures visible changes in the marketplace, leading to a true reflection of the diverse make-up of both Church and society.

The third thing that was bothering me was the 'I'm all right, Jack' attitude, which I recognised in some who could be identified as having middle-class status. Sometimes those who are doing well, who are professionally fluent and involved in society, stand apart, disengaged from the everyday experience of other black people. In terms of public discourse, they're likely to claim, 'There is no problem.' The views of such individuals are amplified in different walks of life. For example, some figures from minority ethnic backgrounds who are living successful lives behave as if they have arrived, suggesting that it's ridiculous to speak of the reality of racism being experienced in Britain today. This needs to be contested.

This problem, of course, doesn't only relate to ethnicity. At some stage, everyone thinks their world is stand-alone, that they are an island. We frequently fail to understand our interconnectedness. A young child growing up will likely be drawn to figures in the field of sport or the music industry, to name but two examples. They'll witness people who look like them building successful careers, and this may prompt them to imagine the role they might inhabit themselves, and to begin to make the necessary arrangements to take them in their chosen direction.

We need to be reminded, however, that though we may be doing well in life – whatever that looks like – it doesn't mean everyone else is too. I'm a firm believer that, on my own, I'm not whole unless all are whole. This means we need to work together so that everyone can become all they can be and achieve their potential.

West Bromwich was a diverse, multi-ethnic, multi-religious and multi-cultural community. As Associate Priest at the Church of the Good Shepherd, I was fortunate to be working in a place with amazing opportunities to walk with everyday people. Great wealth could be found in the quality of family relationships, as well as those across differing neighbourhoods.

One of my joys was taking a weekly assembly in the local authority school. The headmaster was Sikh, and approximately 80% of the children were Muslim, with the other 20% from Hindu, Christian and Sikh backgrounds. I noticed that the Muslim, Sikh and Hindu children were much more articulate about their faith stories than those from Christian families, and more likely to see their religion practised within the home. At Ramadan, for example, young Muslim children would fast during the school day, just as adults fasted while at work. Though I was leading Christian assemblies, I would make connections with other faiths whenever possible, drawing on stories such as Diwali in its teaching of good and evil, light and darkness.

As usual in parish ministry, there were some unexpected moments. One day, I was showing a small and rather timid-looking lady around the church. I wasn't wearing my clerical collar, and after a while of wandering rather aimlessly as I tried to point out things of interest, she plucked up the courage to tell me what was really on her mind.

'My son's getting married, and I've heard that the person doing the ceremony isn't English.'

Knowing exactly where this was heading, I smiled. Allowing myself a brief moment to compose my reply, I hastened to reassure her. 'Actually, I'll be officiating and although I'm from Jamaica originally, I have been properly trained and ordained by the Church of England.' Seeing she was still a bit twitchy, I added, 'And I'll only be using the authorised marriage liturgy of the Church of England.'

She seemed reassured and left. A week or two later, when she approached me after the actual ceremony, I was gratified to hear that she thought the service had been wonderful, and she was sorry she'd ever worried.

Inevitably, as always seemed to be the case when we were just getting settled, Ken had plans of his own. Having gone from a curacy in the town centre church of St Peter's in Wolverhampton to become Vicar of St Andrew's West Bromwich, he was now pondering his next move.

The fact was that Ken had developed a love of prison ministry in his Church Army days, after doing a placement at Strangeways Prison in Manchester. Now he felt he was being led to follow that path. Though this might involve a move that would impact my own work, I knew that enabling Ken to follow his dreams and fulfil his calling was important not only to him, but to us all as a family.

And so, having declared myself willing to support him throughout, we embarked on what turned out to be a long, drawn-out process. On a visit to the then Area Bishop of Stepney, John Sentamu, I told him about Ken's desire for a move. He mentioned that there was a parish in his area that needed a priest and an associate, and although we'd had no plans to work together, Ken and I accepted the invitation to an interview as he'd heard nothing to date from the prison authorities. In my gut, I was unsure if being Ken's associate was the right way forward, but it felt as though we were being guided to explore this parish.

So that's what we set out to do.

14
HACKNEY, HERE I COME!

THE PARISH WAS IN HACKNEY, at the heart of London's East End. It covered Dalston and Haggerston, and Ken and I immediately noticed that there was a lot of regeneration going on. Tower blocks were being pulled down so new houses could be built, and with families moving out to make way for this construction work, the area demographic was beginning to change. Holy Trinity Dalston continued to do reasonably well and had a respectable electoral roll. Its last vicar, Father John, had recently retired to Gloucestershire, and following much consultation, the church had agreed to become a United Benefice with All Saints Haggerston, the next-door parish.

In contrast to Holy Trinity, the number of names on All Saints' electoral roll had fallen drastically. There were now approximately thirty, and on any given Sunday, attendance at the morning service was likely to be between twelve and fifteen people. All Saints had become known as 'the jumble sale church', because every Saturday they would hold a jumble sale. Left-over items were placed in black bags and taken upstairs – filling the balcony. The small proceeds from the sales went to supplement the meagre giving of the congregation.

The local deanery, made up of clergy and laity, had perceived All Saints as not being viable and earmarked it for closure.

It was not a surprising decision given that, both inside and out, the place screamed of struggle and of being unloved. The yard was overgrown. Much of the internal plaster at the east end had fallen off. The carpet was dilapidated and sported burn marks aplenty – as well as years of dripped candlewax. Every part of the church showed signs of DIY work, where someone (I was to learn later that it was the treasurer) had tried to patch things up. He had even added to the existing structure, and while a few minor repairs may not have needed clearance from the church authorities, putting in a new toilet without faculty permission was most definitely not allowed! Something was obviously very wrong with the All Saints administration, and that suggested a clear breakdown of communication at both local and diocesan level.

In the more formal interview that followed our quick scout round the parish, Ken and I found the representatives from Holy Trinity warm, relaxed and welcoming. Two of those from All Saints, on the other hand, appeared suspicious and closed. Perhaps, given the threat hanging over their church, we were viewed as those who might wield the axe of closure. In fact, if they'd raised the topic, I could have reassured them that closure was far from my mind! It was obvious to me that this area – which, unlike other parts of Hackney, could not be described as predominantly Jewish or Muslim – was ripe for evangelism.

On the journey back to the Midlands, Ken was a little bit pensive.

'Well,' I said, 'what did you think? How did you feel the interview went?'

'I don't think this job is for me. It's all very challenging. I don't think I have it in me to meet the challenge.'

I could appreciate what he was saying. The cost of carrying out the necessary repairs and restoration on All Saints alone would be approximately quarter of a million pounds. We would need to grow the congregation alongside fundraising for the money to do the building works.

'This really isn't the job for me,' Ken repeated.

Almost before he'd finished speaking, I surprised myself by saying, 'I'd love the challenge – if they'll have me!'

When we got home, I wrote to Bishop John Sentamu. I was careful with my wording and shared that Ken didn't feel the post was the right one for him before going on to repeat that I would be ready to welcome such a challenge, if he'd have me.

Bishop John's response was encouraging and positive. However, All Saints was a Crown Appointment, and some time elapsed before I was eventually invited to the necessary meeting with the representative from the Prime Minister's office. His warm welcome really did put me at ease during what felt more like a conversation than an interview. He ended our time together by informing me that the people from All Saints would like to see me again. Apparently, they were unsure what my vision for the church might be and wanted to hear more.

I was aware that a neighbouring Forward in Faith[1] church was trying to entice All Saints to join their movement. If they did so, a woman would be off the table as a suitable appointee. I'd also heard they were uncomfortable about the colour of my skin. It seemed prudent, therefore, to respond

---

1 Forward in Faith (FiF) is an organisation operating in the Church of England, a tradition-alist group characterised by its opposition to the ordination of women to the priesthood and the episcopate.

by saying that I was more interested in learning about their vision for the church and how I might help enact this. Also, feeling prompted to be bold, I told the PM's representative that I was not prepared to be re-interviewed by the folk from All Saints. I said I believed there were other agendas at play, and though I made no hint that the colour of my skin might be a factor (I refused to dignify such prejudice by articulating it), it was most certainly implied.

I continued, 'You are interviewing me now, so you must decide if you think I am the right person for the role.' And when he didn't respond: 'So as not to leave you in any doubt where I stand, I would be happy to accept the role if it was offered.'

I returned home, waited, and eventually a letter arrived. The post was mine to accept! However, there was still a lot to be smoothed out. Ken, in the meantime, had been invited to explore a deputy prison chaplain role at Pentonville Prison. He was to start before I was up and running.

While she was still at primary school, Ken had begun buying Amanda boarding school stories, such as Enid Blyton's Malory Towers series. The books featured girls who were always having fun and adventures, and Ken thought they might encourage her to think about boarding during her secondary school years. Having visited some of the local secondary schools in our area, I was shocked by the lack of discipline and the failure to address things such as swearing, furniture being thrown around and the fact that some children simply refused to follow simple instructions. I knew first-hand the impact this kind of behaviour could have on learning. Although we did not believe in paying for education, Ken and I felt we could not put our children into such a system. So, having had a good look around, we chose Tettenhall College, an Anglican foundation educational establishment with a good record of all-round achievement.

Amanda was now settled as a weekly boarder, but the move to London would necessitate her boarding full-time, returning home only at half-term and for the holidays. The fact is, although we did our best to prepare them, we didn't fully appreciate until later how big a deal packing up home and moving was going to be for the children. There would be reverberations in the future.

All three came with us to look at primary schools in Hackney for Hannah and Jamie. In one, as the head teacher was showing us around, she mentioned that the children were encouraged to call their teachers by their first name.

Amanda piped up immediately, 'My mother won't like that.'

I was thrilled she had the confidence to make herself heard. Continuing our tour, I noticed that the pictures on each classroom door showed images of little black girls and boys. I remember thinking that culturally these children would not normally be allowed to call the adults around them by their first name. I was saddened that this cultural norm was not being respected, and felt this was one of many challenges being faced within the local community that we would only be able to mitigate by the grace of God.

Even as I waited for the final arrangements to be put in place in Hackney, I was planning our farewell at the local church in West Bromwich. It was not easy to detach ourselves from the Diocese of Lichfield, which had said yes to me and allowed my ordained ministry to be birthed. It felt a bit like leaving the nest. But time was moving on and we'd been called to move on too.

Eventually, all the relevant diaries were able to find a suitable date in April 1998 to hold my licensing service. My meeting with the wardens and priest-in-charge for preliminary discussions hinted there would be more challenges ahead. The priest had decided that he did not want to be present for my first service at All Saints, and had invited a visiting minister to lead instead. I was uncomfortable about this, as I felt it was important to start in both churches on the same Sunday. So I asked him to cancel the invitation. What this meant was that, as I was leading the whole service, I would not be able to stay behind at Holy Trinity (where the service began at 9:30 a.m.) to meet with members, as it would be rude not to be at All Saints in good time for their 11 a.m. start. Fortunately, everyone at the meeting seemed happy to agree that we should try to create regular opportunities for social gatherings so we could get to know one another.

Following my first Sunday in the parish, I met with all four churchwardens. One of the two from All Saints said in a very abrupt manner, 'The reason there were so many people at your first service was because we were expecting a male priest [the original arrangement]. We were rather put out to see you there.'

I was taken aback, but took a deep breath and proceeded to share what I really thought, albeit with more gentleness than I was feeling. 'As you're keen to put your cards on the table, why don't you lay them all out? Has it got anything to do with the fact that I am black?'

At least the response I got from one of them was honest: 'Well, frankly, yes!'

I took another deep breath. 'Now that you've put your cards on the table, let me put my cards on the table too. I have only just arrived here. I am very happy in my skin and in my gender and I have no intention of going anywhere. But if you or anyone else is unhappy with me because I am black or because I am a woman, you are free to go.'

That meeting was the start of a series of troublesome interactions with key people within the leadership of All Saints Church. It would have been better if they had taken me up on my offer and departed immediately, but they didn't, orchestrating many difficulties instead.

As the incumbent, I was in a position of leadership, and I made the conscious decision that it wouldn't be right – in fact, it might be positively harmful – to bring an associate priest into such an unstable environment. Repeatedly, the All Saints churchwardens would ask, 'Where is our priest? We were promised another priest!' I would reply that I was their priest.

Eventually I had to spell things out even more clearly. 'The reason you're asking about another priest is because you want a priest who is male and white. That would enable you to say, "We don't need to acknowledge her; we can ignore her." Well,' I said, banging my hand on the nearby lectern (the only occasion I have ever banged my hand on an object while speaking to adult congregants), 'I will not be ignored in my church!'

Reflecting on this fraught situation, I realise such a possessive way of speaking – which I frequently advise others to avoid! – wasn't necessarily helpful, and I still feel somewhat embarrassed about it. After all, the church was God's, not mine.

Deep in my heart I was convinced this was where God was calling me to be. Yet in those early months, to be frank, I felt unsafe. What made things worse was that I didn't feel able to share this with anyone, because if I had, they'd probably have thought I wasn't coping. I was having a gut reaction to the fact that these people, who did not want me there, were behaving in an irrational manner. So, my subconscious reasoned, what was to stop them doing me some kind of unimaginable harm? Perhaps I too was becoming irrational! The one person I could bear my soul to was God. So I turned, in my troubles, to a traditional song from my childhood days, 'Jesus, be a fence'. I felt comforted by that song, in which I was really asking for God's constant protection. It became a prayer that I sang several times per day.

Notwithstanding the continuing challenges, I found the gritty ministry I was engaged in deeply fulfilling. Holy Trinity and All Saints had drawn in many who were profoundly grateful for all God had made possible for them and their families. Conscious of their lack of possessions, they knew, spiritually, that all would be well. I was reminded of the kind of trust I'd seen displayed during my childhood by very ordinary people who became extraordinary due to their reliance on a greater power beyond themselves.

One parishioner in Hackney who made quite an impression on me was a woman from the Caribbean country of Belize. She'd met and fallen in love with a young British soldier while he was on a tour of duty in her country. They'd approached the local expat priest from the United Kingdom, who was unable to hide his disdain at their being together. One of the questions her future husband had been asked was how he'd feel waking up next to a black woman every morning!

Against the odds, this couple made London their home and had a long and successful marriage. He attended worship with his grandchildren and, as she was now wheelchair bound, I'd take Holy Communion to her at home every week.

I had noticed that the parents and grandparents of African and Caribbean heritage were more likely to bring their grandchildren to church than their white counterparts. Nellie Brown (in a neighbouring church) was one such grandmother …

In 2004, I watched her and her family, while deep in grief, react with compassion towards the young man who had contributed to the death of her grandson, Robert Levy. As was reported in the national press at the time, Robert, while only yards from his home in Hackney, had attempted to break up a fight between two fourteen-year-old boys. Robert's bravery resulted in him being fatally stabbed by one of them. At the time, I remembered thinking that the inaction of the adults who walked on by without speaking to the two boys contributed to Robert's death.

Nellie was a real woman of prayer. Her generosity of spirit in the face of this tragedy, and the enthusiasm with which she engaged in worship, were a living testimony to all that God had done in the lives of her family.

I learned very quickly that the older women of the parish, who were originally from a variety of different countries, saw me as their daughter. For those of my age group, I was their sister, while young adults referred to me as Aunty. The love these women displayed, as they embraced me and my ministry, allowed me to overcome the negativity of those blinded by racism. Hackney will always have a special place in my heart.

On one occasion, I remember calling a cab en route to a speaking engagement. Arriving at King's Cross Station, I discovered to my horror that I'd left my purse behind and had no money to pay the taxi driver, whom I'd never met, nor any credit cards to purchase my ticket to Cambridge. I was astonished when the driver said, 'Don't worry. Here's some money to carry you over. You can let me have it back in the week.' Mr Bola had given me enough for the train fare and a taxi at the other end. He was Nigerian, a Muslim, and the 'senior brother' in his family. Our long association remained strong throughout my time in Hackney, with our taxi conversations ranging across faith, family and politics. He wasn't afraid to ask for prayers in difficult family circumstances either.

Engaging with the local shopkeepers also came naturally. I remember being interviewed by Jeremy Vine as he was recording a programme for Radio 4. It involved us chatting while walking around the parish. In one shop, the Muslim proprietor told him I was their priest! They may not have been members of my congregation, but these shopkeepers were part of my parish. They were individuals who knew I cared for them just as much as I cared for any confirmed or regular attenders at church. They respected the fact that I treated them and their faith with respect, never trying to proselytise them, but instead trying to introduce them, through my actions, to the God of love I served.

It was while we were still in Hackney that I became known as 'the vicar on the roof'. It happened like this …

We'd had a very heavy downpour, and I thought I should probably check all was well at All Saints. It wasn't! Entering the church, I discovered water pouring onto the floor.

My immediate response was frustration: although money was being invested in the community, the church – its largest building – was not getting any of this to assist with repairs. Yet when there was any significant crisis in the country, it was to the church that many turned for comfort. I decided in the heat of the moment that I would draw people's attention to the fact that All Saints was being neglected, by climbing onto the roof – and remaining there for twenty-four hours.

The curate, Richenda, decided to join me. I had not immediately disclosed that we were going to fast throughout our protest, and it was only when a curry takeaway arrived that I broke the news to her. She took it well! The press got wind of our exploits and in no time at all Ken was climbing the ladder with the phone so I could make the most of the publicity we were attracting. A visiting television crew ensured we made the lunchtime and evening news. The money started pouring in (much as the rain had), and with people calling from as far afield as Canada – and many locals coming to view us and donate too – we raised approximately £25,000. When I discovered that so many people had responded to our appeal, I said to Ken that I wished I had stayed on the roof longer!

My final major fundraising effort – skydiving – was no less exhilarating. Finding myself in an airfield in Cambridgeshire accompanied by members of my congregation to cheer me on, I turned to the chap with whom I'd be jumping in tandem. I told him I wanted to make sure he was happy and loved his life! With good weather, we prepared for the jump. I was sitting on the lap of my newly found partner, and when it was our turn we shuffled to the end of the plane. With a simple tap on the shoulder, we were off, and began to descend. I remember praying the Lord's Prayer, consciously aware of the 'out of this world experience' I was having. When I got to the ground, I promised Ken I would make sure I took out insurance before doing something as crazy as skydiving again.

I'm not sure he believed me!

15
ROYAL CONNECTIONS

ON A CHILLY DECEMBER EVENING in 2007, I got home to the news that Christopher Hill, the Bishop of Guildford, had been trying to reach me. I remember feeling puzzled as to why, before figuring the likely explanation was that he wanted to offer me a job in his diocese. As I knew it wasn't yet the right time to leave Hackney, there seemed little point in returning the call.

I was quite unaware that as well as being Bishop of Guildford, Christopher carried another responsibility: he was 'Clerk of the Closet'. (In this role, he looked after the royal chaplains and was, in effect, part of the ecclesiastical household.) So, when the phone rang again the following Saturday, I picked it up casually – this was the weekend, after all – with no notion of what was about to ensue.

'I have been trying to reach you,' said the bishop.

'Yes,' I replied and proceeded to explain why I had not got back to him.

Imagine my surprise when he revealed the purpose of his call was to tell me that the Queen would love me to become one of her chaplains.

'You are joking, aren't you?' (I was in shock!)

'You should have received a letter in the post, inviting you.'

The letter duly arrived on Monday morning. And within days I had another phone call.

On this occasion, the person on the other end claimed to be ringing from Buckingham Palace. He told me that Her Majesty the Queen and the Duke of Edinburgh would love to have me and my husband for dinner and an overnight stay at Windsor Castle. My immediate thought was that someone who'd heard of the new appointment was playing a prank. So when the caller asked me to take down a number to use if I had any questions, I did so while telling myself I would not ring it. I did not want to give anyone the satisfaction of believing I'd been fooled!

Yet, lo and behold, a few days later a second letter arrived. Like the first, it had ER (Elizabeth Regina) stamped in red on the envelope, and as I read it carefully over and over again, in case this was some even more elaborate hoax, I couldn't stop asking myself: how could it be that this little girl who'd grown up in Montego Bay was being invited to dine with the Queen of England?

The evening before the big day, Ken and I packed with some excitement. We were amused that the paperwork stated accommodation would be provided at the castle for my chauffeur and, in jest, I suggested Ken come in that role! Of course, I drove myself, with my dear husband reminding me from time to time to keep an eye on the speedometer.

On arrival, we were given directions and told that tea would be served shortly. Our bags, in the meantime, would be carried inside. The Duke of Edinburgh had only just returned from a short spell in hospital, and we were informed that he would not be at dinner, but happily he did join us briefly for tea. Her Majesty moved easily around the small, intimate gathering, and when she reached me I shared with her the headline that had appeared in a newspaper back home regarding my appointment: 'A Jamaican Rose in the Queen's Garden!' She was clearly amused by this. I listened as she conversed with Ken about his current role and shared something of Princess Anne's work in prisons. I remembered thinking, *Wow, she really knows about her children's concerns!* More importantly, it was clear from the fond way she spoke of them that she was genuinely interested in what they were doing.

That day cemented things for me. From then on, I regarded Her Majesty first and foremost as a mother, then a grandmother, a great-grandmother and a wife; being Queen Elizabeth II came after all those roles. I respected her for having navigated 'a man's world' and for all those years of sometimes being the only woman in the room, or the only woman at the table. On many occasions, world leaders, presidents and prime ministers – some self-proclaimed, some duly elected – would have had to listen to her address them, whether they wanted to or not. Having been crowned at such a young, impressionable age, I was full of admiration for how she had managed to keep going when surrounded by men with a sense of entitlement, no doubt keen to give her their advice.

Both Ken and I were assigned an assistant. Ken's insisted on cleaning his shoes, even though Ken pointed out that he had actually performed this task himself earlier in the day. He obligingly removed his shoes nevertheless, only to have the assistant return a moment or two later, saying, 'I'm afraid I can't improve them, sir.'

My female assistant quite unexpectedly asked, 'May I run a bath for you, my lady?'

I thanked her in some awe and went on to enjoy the bath. This was indeed another world – very pleasant to inhabit, even if only momentarily. The apartment we were assigned only added to the sense of unreality, as there were several artefacts that we presumed had been given as gifts to the Queen from overseas visitors – or perhaps brought back from her many overseas tours.

I had packed two dresses, unsure which I would end up choosing for the evening meal. In the event, I decided against the one I'd gone out and bought days before, and it's still in my wardrobe, unworn to this day! I wasn't convinced it was a comfortable enough fit for such a special occasion and, for me, being comfortable means not having to worry about how my dress is looking. A parishioner had kindly made some minor adjustments to my other option – previously worn to a wedding – and with it on, I felt calm and relaxed. Ken, in evening dress, looked sharp (as we'd say in Jamaica)! My handsome husband and I duly stepped out to join Her Majesty and the other invited dinner guests.

Over several courses with accompanying wine, conversations were orderly as, taking our cue from the Queen, we spoke first to the person on our right – for me, Prince Edward, who was placed opposite his mother – and then to the person on our left. After dinner, Her Majesty invited the ladies on a personal tour of selected parts of the castle, including the chapel. She spoke movingly of the fire that had devastated her much-loved home in November 1992, and of the painstaking work to restore it afterwards. When we got to the library, it was clear that researchers had been asked to display pieces of work that had some significance for each guest. The Queen spoke to me about documents on the disestablishment of the Church of England from Jamaica in 1870, and I marvelled at the way she had made the visit so interesting for everyone there. All in all, it was something pretty amazing to share with my grandchildren in years to come!

Later, when Ken and I returned to the apartment we'd been given, we noted that our night clothes had been laid out on our respective beds in two separate rooms. A quick exchange of glances confirmed we knew instinctively we would be breaking this one unspoken house rule! The next morning, waking up as man and wife in the same bed, we heard a knock on the door. The lady assigned to me entered carrying a tray laden with tea and orange juice. If she was shocked to find Ken there too (well covered by the sheets as he was), her facial expression gave no sign.

It was a pleasure to join the other guests for a full English breakfast, with a couple of corgis pottering around as we ate at our leisure. I wondered if anyone might try to slip them something tasty, but we were as well behaved as they were. Soon it was time to say our farewells, and we arrived outside to find that our car had been returned from its valet parking and was now on the driveway with our luggage stowed inside. I nimbly got into the driver's seat! Smiling at each other as we pondered all that had happened over the last few hours, Ken and I knew we had had the experience of a lifetime, and what was most important was that we had shared it together.

The following summer, at the Royal Garden Party, the new chaplains were to be presented formally to Her Majesty. It was particularly nice in this instance to be allowed to drive right into the palace forecourt. Currently, due to fear of terrorist attack, parking along The Mall has been discontinued, and everyone is expected to arrive by public transport. This is not ideal if you're all dressed up in your most special attire. I am enormously thankful that we as Queen's Chaplains are allowed to attend in our scarlet cassocks. And now, as a bishop, I wear a purple cassock. This has proved a real godsend. First, I don't have to fuss about finding a special garden party outfit, and second, I can wear flat shoes! Instead of having heels sinking into the palace lawn as I walk, or trying to balance elegantly as I stand, I can enjoy these beautiful events in comfort.

Back in 2008, we took our places in the line-up that precedes entry to the royal tea tent. The Duke of Edinburgh moved across to our daughters, and with his usual dry sense of humour asked, 'What are your parents feeding you on?' This brought smiles to their faces and to those of many around them. The fact is that the girls are stunningly tall! Following this formality, my family and I were invited into the tent, where we happily conversed with other members of the royal family, and mingled with an intriguing gathering of fellow guests.

One spring Saturday morning in 2018, Ken and I were strolling to the market when my phone rang. The caller told me that Prince Harry and Meghan Markle had asked if I would lead prayers at their forthcoming wedding. This was a great surprise and I accepted the invitation with much joy. However, I could say nothing until the order of service was released, just before the ceremony itself. It was only then that the wider world could see who was taking part.

I found it a real privilege to be part of such a special moment in the lives of this young couple. Yet what was particularly exciting – as I love to tell the children I visit in primary schools – was being driven in a convoy from London to Windsor surrounded by police outriders!

This would not be my only experience of being escorted thus … In May 2023, it became clear that a long-term, Covid-delayed engagement to speak in New York was going to clash with the coronation of King Charles III. I'd been told in February to keep myself available for the date of the coronation as I was down to do 'a little something'. Again, I was excited but unable to tell anyone. However, as the date of the coronation drew near and nothing else was said about my involvement, I began to think that I may not have heard correctly in the first place. Maybe the hint was a figment of my imagination! I pondered how to check this out without looking like a fool, but in the end the best thing seemed simply to ask. Plucking up my courage, I learned to my relief that I did indeed have a role: that of processing with the patten (a eucharistic vessel) that would be used for Holy Communion during the service. Guli Francis-Dehqani, the Bishop of Chelmsford, would be processing with the chalice, another eucharistic vessel.

This did, however, leave me with the problem of needing to change the dates of my New York trip. I would no longer be there for two weekends as originally planned – a real disappointment as I had invitations to preach at the Cathedral of St John the Divine on the first weekend and St Thomas Church, also in Manhattan, on the second weekend. After much discussion, it was agreed that I would attend both churches on the same day, preaching at St Thomas in the morning and at St John the Divine at evensong, when I would have the added pleasure of being installed in the ecumenical seat of the cathedral. My only other engagement – and the main reason for my visit – was to address the Church Club of New York. Everything seemed to be fitting into place. However, with less than a month to go, rehearsal dates for the coronation were distributed, and I discovered there was to be a dress rehearsal on Thursday 4th, two days before the coronation itself – the same date I was booked to fly out of New York. With some trepidation, I approached the organisers about the possibility of catching a flight straight after my address on the evening of Wednesday 3rd. This meant I had to explain why such a rapid exit would be necessary. But they were very helpful and understanding, and promised not to reveal anything until the appropriate announcement had been made in the UK.

On the night in question, one of the attendees at my table shared her concern about possible delays getting to the airport. She proceeded to contact the NYPD (New York Police Department) to ask if they would provide an escort. They replied that they would drive Ken and me themselves! A very pleasant young officer appeared, and we headed off with flashing lights and sirens. Twice when vehicles did not move out of our lane quickly enough, he proceeded to use his megaphone to order, 'Move to the right, now!' and the instruction was obeyed just as soon as it was given.

The officer told me that he would be watching the coronation with his family. I said he could tell them he'd made it possible for me to get back for it in time! Arriving at JFK, we were warmly greeted by airport staff, and I discovered I'd been upgraded to first class for the journey home.

We touched down at Heathrow at 11:30 a.m. and after clearing customs and collecting our bags headed for the Heathrow Express train, which gets to central London in a mere fifteen minutes. From there a cab transported us to the hotel that had been booked for the bishops who would be taking part in the service. After quickly freshening up, I headed to Westminster Abbey to be robed up ready for the dress rehearsal. There was a buzz both outside and inside the abbey by now, with the world's press present and already running storylines from a variety of angles. There were several requests for me to do interviews, and the national comms team helped me be selective. I really appreciated this as I was quite tired after my long journey, having been much too keyed up to fall into a deep sleep.

All the spouses who had not been invited to the coronation service were welcome to attend the dress rehearsal. It did not go entirely smoothly, and a few people stayed behind to have another run through. I needed to rest! I headed back to the hotel, while Ken travelled down to Kent, as he wanted to watch the service on the big screen surrounded by his home comforts rather than alone in a hotel room. I was sad he could not be with me on the day. When Queen Elizabeth II was crowned, over 8,000 guests filled the abbey. But these days, health and safety guidelines simply do not allow so many guests to be crammed into an ancient building. The pressure on space meant that the spouses and partners of those taking part – even the archbishops' wives – could not attend the service, however much Their Majesties may have wished it otherwise.

I am not convinced I got any sleep at all the night before the coronation, though this was probably due less to anxiety than to excitement. I was like a child awaiting Christmas, counting down every hour that came and went. As dawn broke, I rose to say my prayers and then headed down for breakfast – not because I was hungry but as a way of keeping my thoughts occupied. I had been briefed that there were several requests for press interviews before the service. After robing, I made my way to Lambeth Palace where the one interview I had accepted would take place. There would be others, previously agreed, after the service. Even as we (the bishops taking part) set out together from Lambeth Palace through the cordons, several individuals from the independent press vied for our attention. We mostly smiled as we walked purposefully to Westminster Abbey.

Bishop Guli and I then made our way to our designated area in the cloisters. With us was the Bishop of Jerusalem, Archbishop Hosam. He would process with the actual Bible on which the King would swear the coronation oath, and during the service would present the Archbishop of Canterbury with oil to anoint the King. We also had the Lord High Steward of England, General Sir Gordon Messenger KCB DSO OBE carrying the St Edward's Crown (several of us made use of this once-in-a-lifetime opportunity to be photographed next to it!); Baroness Benjamin OM DBE DL (fondly remembered by children growing up in the 1970s and 80s as Floella on BBC1's *Playschool*) carrying the King's sceptre, and Dame Elizabeth Anionwu OM DBE carrying the orb. As already mentioned, Bishop Guli would bear the chalice and I the patten. All four of us women in the procession were from global majority heritage backgrounds and would be making history, not only by our presence but also by our engagement in the service. This coronation would thus be very different from that of Queen Elizabeth II, seventy-one years earlier.

I was deeply touched that Queen Camilla had specifically asked for the Bishop of Dover to present her with the rod, an item of her regalia. Here I was, this girl from Montego Bay, about to be visibly engaged at the very heart of the institution of the monarchy.

As we began to process along the short route through the cloisters and into the abbey, I felt somewhat lost in the moment – it was as if I were a character in the unfolding tale of a storybook. To pull myself together, I intentionally looked around on entering the abbey and was glad to find myself recognising several faces; reassuringly they responded to my smile. Finally reaching my place, I settled down briefly before the fanfare sounded that got everyone in the abbey up on their feet. Their Majesties had arrived! The music was extraordinarily moving as they made their way down the aisle.

Many have since spoken of the ceremony and what it meant to them. My response has always been that it was an intrinsically religious service, in which both the King and the Queen were consecrated and set apart for service, solemnly blessed for their royal duties. They made a commitment to serve the people of the United Kingdom and the Commonwealth. The context of the ceremony was the Eucharist, and taking Holy Communion that day were the Archbishop of Canterbury, myself, Bishop Guli and the King and Queen (in that order!). I could see that both Their Majesties were profoundly moved by the service, and the tenderness with which Prince William kissed his father was deeply touching.

Afterwards, once outside the abbey, Bishop Guli and I made our way through the crowds to our various media interviews. These immediately went viral, with family, friends and other folks in Jamaica and the USA quickly getting in touch and sending lots of screen shots to my phone! Then, when we'd collected our luggage, we set off for the tube station only to find the nearest ones (Westminster, St James's Park, Embankment and Charing Cross) were all closed, as literally thousands of people attempted to make their way home. After walking some distance, Bishop Guli and I parted company, and I continued my journey to Piccadilly and the opulent eighteenth-century department store, Fortnum & Mason.

I had been invited to high tea, for which the store is deservedly famous, and among the guests were Katy Perry, Edward Enninful, Vanessa Kingori and Lionel Richie. My friends Paulette and Eva, members of the gospel choir that performed at the service, and advocates of the Prince's Trust, had been invited too. This day just kept on giving … I later learned that Jayden, my oldest grandson, was most impressed that I got to meet Katy Perry. My wow moment, though, was speaking with Lionel Richie. I had danced to so many of his songs through the years, so it was absolutely fabulous to be in the room with him!

As we left Fortnum & Mason, there was still a great buzz in the air, with many people greeting me and saying they had seen me on the screen while watching the service.

Just over a month later, I met the King while attending the unveiling of the exhibition 'Windrush: Portraits of a Pioneering Generation'. He asked if I had got over the coronation.

'No,' I said. 'I am holding it in my left hand, and in the right hand I am getting on with life. Every so often I look at the left hand, pinching myself and reliving a little bit of the history of that day and the occasion.'

So many millions of people watched the coronation that not a week goes by without someone commenting to me about it. What warms my heart is hearing, 'Because you were there, we felt that we were represented.' These words have come from people all over Kent, as well as from the places where I previously served, in Hackney, north-east London and the Midlands.

King Charles succeeded his mother by virtue of his birth. In interviews leading up to the coronation, I was asked on several occasions, 'Do you think he will be able to step into his mother's shoes?'

Each time my reply was, 'No, it is important that he wears his own shoes, as trying to fit in someone else's can be very uncomfortable. He will wear his own shoes and do the best job he can.'

I have met so many young people whose lives have been changed and who credit the change to the support of the Prince's Trust, founded by the then Prince Charles in 1976. I believe that sends a strong signal as to the kind of monarch we have been blessed with.

Long live the King!

16

CHAPLAIN TO THE SPEAKER OF THE HOUSE OF COMMONS

PART 1

IN THE AUTUMN OF 2009, it began to feel as if my ministry in Hackney might be coming to an end. A great deal had happened in the last ten years: the congregation had grown and changed, with many who had been little more than children when I arrived beginning to have families of their own. I was baptising their offspring, then seeing them start at the same school where I had led hundreds of assemblies and even taught from time to time. I loved the people of the parish, and they loved me. The thought of leaving was painful to contemplate, yet I knew I could not allow feelings of pending loss to prevent me from exploring other areas of ministry experience.

Annual visits to Jamaica were always lifegiving for me. Sometimes all the family would accompany me; sometimes I would make a short visit on my own. I remember Ken once remarking that we were not likely to see many other countries because every time I had a break, I wanted to go to Jamaica! I never really thought of it this way. I just knew how much I was fed by staying connected to the people and the soil I held so dearly.

It was while I was on one of these solo visits to family and friends that I had a call from Ken to say he had seen an interesting job going in the *Church Times*. It was advertised in three parts: Canon at Westminster Abbey, Rector of St Margaret's Church (the small church alongside the abbey) and Chaplain to the Speaker of the House of Commons. Ken had hardly finished speaking when I responded: 'I want real work. Walking around wearing red robes is not my idea of real work.'

My response was not meant to be disrespectful to those who held such posts. I simply wanted something that would be challenging and tough; something that would match the gritty kind of work I had been doing in Hackney and, before then, in the Midlands. In all my roles up to this point, my ministry had made a difference: I was creating change and sometimes being the change I wanted to see. I was keen to continue doing so. Ken understood this and no more was said. I would simply keep looking each week at the job advertisements and praying to discern what God had in store for me.

A week or two after I returned to London, I bumped into a couple of ministry colleagues, April Alexander and Ian Harper. Each, independent of the other, said to me: 'Rose, have you seen the job going at the abbey? I think you should apply for it.'

I recall thinking how strange it was that two priests from an evangelical background would direct me towards such a role. However, I knew that April and Ian were both exceptionally committed to a life of prayer; God might just be seeking to say something to me through them! I decided to go on the internet and read up about the job. That was when I really noticed the 'Chaplain to the Speaker' element. The words seemed to lift off the screen. Immediately, I thought, *Faith needs to be in the public square confidently and unapologetically, and I want to be a part of that.* I felt excitement rising at the prospect of such a challenge and, after much prayer and encouragement from Ken, decided that it would be right to apply for the job.

In arriving at this decision, I felt it was important to ring the abbey and speak to the Dean, John Hall, whom I knew from attending various events.

'I've seen the advert,' I said, 'and I thought I would ask if you're interested in women applying for the role. Completing applications for jobs like these is like writing a book, and I don't want to spend hours filling out a form if the answer is no.'

'I'm very keen for women to apply,' he replied. 'As a matter of fact, I gave advance notice to the Dean of Women's Ministry by asking for it to be passed around to the senior women in the diocese.'

His response left me puzzled. The senior women of the diocese met at St Paul's Cathedral around twice a year. How was it then that this information had never been shared with me? Had someone already decided I wasn't suited to the role? I couldn't help but smile; whatever issue lay behind this, it would simply spur me on! The words of the Labi Siffre song 'Something Inside so Strong' came to life for me as I focused on working through the application.

However, when it came to references, there was a hitch. One of the referees was to be my bishop and, at the time, the Bishop of Stepney was on compassionate leave. I turned to the Bishop of London, who explained that he was already acting as a referee for other priests applying for the same job. Why did I feel that there was another message being given to me, such as: 'Don't bother; this is a waste of time'? I told him that I did not have a choice, as my area bishop was unavailable and a bishop's reference was required. Promising to send him my CV in case he needed more on my background, I decided to hand deliver this and the application personally. I didn't want to risk sending it through the post in case it got lost.

Time was now of the essence. Nonetheless, I hoped it might be possible to fit in a meeting and discussion with the person who currently held the role. Unfortunately, due to commitments I'd made to my congregations and the lack of space in his diary, this wasn't possible prior to me being shortlisted. After I was shortlisted, he was reluctant to see me. I believe he thought doing so might be seen as giving me an advantage. I was disappointed by this response. Yet I accepted the decision was out of my hands. Now all I needed to do was pray, prepare and wait for the interview in April 2010.

It was to take place over two days. The six of us who were shortlisted – four men and two women – met with the Dean in his study, accompanied by our spouses. He revealed that ninety-seven people had applied for the job! We were shown around the abbey and the residence. Then, as part of the interview process, we were taken across to Parliament, where we each had approximately three minutes with the Speaker, John Bercow, in his office.

The next day we were on our own. The actual interview I thought went well. On the panel were John Hall (the Dean), Douglas Hurd (the former Foreign Secretary, now serving in the Lords), Caroline Boddington (the Archbishops' Secretary for Appointments), Robert Keys MP (representing the Speaker) and Sir Paul Britton (Appointments Secretary to the Prime Minister). I was not altogether relaxed, but I had prayed, others were praying, and I felt as if I were in the hands of God. I trusted him and believed that if it was his will, then all would be well. We have a saying in Jamaica, 'Wah a fi yuh a fi yuh! No baddy can tek I weh!' (What is yours is yours. No one can take it away from you!) So I was not going to worry. What would be would be. After all, no one was pushing me away from Hackney. I was at peace.

At the end of the interview process, we were told that the Speaker would be consulted and we'd hear further the following day. Late the next morning, I had a call from someone telling me that they had still not managed to consult with the Speaker, and as it was now the half-term break, there would be a short delay. I simply said, 'No problem,' and left it at that. The next week came and went and there was no more contact.

By the following Monday, I was beginning to feel somewhat unsettled. Whether or not they had appointed someone – and it was all right if they had – I would be glad to have some kind of news or feedback. I waited with as much patience as I could muster through Tuesday, Wednesday and Thursday. Then on Friday, mid-morning, the phone rang. I was told – I assumed by the same person who had called me before – that a decision had still not been made.

I responded, 'That's OK. I thought you had already appointed someone, and I was planning to be in touch with you for some feedback regarding the interview.'

We hung up. I was conscious now of feeling rather pensive. When I thought they'd already made a decision, I had been very much at peace because, after all, I was not entitled to the role. Now that I knew there was still a chance, I wanted to keep hope alive and pray more fervently about it!

Approximately half an hour later, my caller rang back. 'Do you know what's happening?' he asked.

'No,' I said, and repeated, 'I thought it had already been decided, but I would like some feedback on the interview.'

'Well, let me explain. The abbey do not think you are the right person for them, but we would like to have you here in Parliament.'

Wow, I thought, *I am still in the mix for this role!*

'What if we were to split the job ... would you still consider taking it?'

Without hesitation I responded, 'I would love to. It was the Parliamentary part that drew my interest in the post.'

'OK,' he said, 'I will be back in touch with regard to taking the new offer forward.'

I did not realise it then, but I was setting out on an exceptional journey – and there would be a torrent of challenges to come. The words given to me on that poster at the Church Army college seemed to be coming into their own:

'Do not go where the path leads. Go where there is no path and leave a trail.'

I was going to be the first ever woman Chaplain to the Speaker of the House of Commons!

My excitement was mingled with some uncertainty. There was no accommodation provided with the role, as the residence we had been shown would be offered to the colleague who was becoming Canon of Westminster Abbey and Rector of St Margaret's. This meant that I could not move physically from my parish in Hackney unless I sourced another part-time role, with accommodation, preferably in the City and within easy reach of Westminster. I've no memory of anyone at diocesan leadership level offering any useful suggestions in this regard, or indeed of congratulating me on my appointment.

When the press got hold of the news, they seemed determined to paint a picture of a Speaker who was going off piste, who was concerned to be politically correct. In other words, the message was that the new appointee had not been chosen because she was competent and qualified for the job but because she was a woman and a black woman.

One newspaper described my colleague who got the role at the abbey and St Margaret's as 'the Oxford graduate'. There was nothing in my brief portrayal to indicate that I too had a degree. Instead, I was called 'the girl from Montego Bay'. It was at that moment I vowed that if I ever wrote my autobiography, it would be called *The Girl from Montego Bay*!

Some months after I began working in Parliament, John Bercow and I had a conversation in which we reflected on the furore around my appointment. He shared with me not only that my paperwork had merited me being shortlisted, but these thrilling words: 'You walked into my office. You had presence. You were dynamic. I just had to have you.'

I will never forget such a vote of confidence. He believed in me and was always supportive. We had a great working relationship, and we're still in touch. I continue to hold him and his family in my prayers.

Once I was able to share the predicament I was in with my churchwardens and PCC, they gave permission for me to stay on in Hackney for the foreseeable future, thrilled not to be losing me just yet. Touchingly, it was not only members of my congregation who expressed their delight in my new position, but also local folk in the wider parish who had no affiliation with the church at all. They regarded me as one of their own, and it was in that capacity I would be taking on this significant post. I am greatly indebted to the people of my church and the local community who loved me unconditionally, supported me, told me, 'You can!' and made it possible for me to inhabit the new role while continuing to minister to them for a further four years.

Of course, continuing my parish work while getting to grips with the new job was challenging. But it mattered to me that I met every deadline. I would be conducting funerals, officiating at other services and hosting meetings, while running backwards and forwards, in and out of Westminster every day.

My chaplaincy involved leading prayers in the parliamentary chambers on all the days the House was sitting; officiating at weddings and baptisms in the Chapel of St Mary Undercroft, and caring pastorally for those on the parliamentary estate (the parliamentarians in both Houses; the security team; the administrative, catering and cleaning staff). I did this, in the main, simply by getting alongside them. The administrative support my predecessor in the role had enjoyed had been withdrawn, but with or without it I was going to rise to the occasion. To be frank, I sometimes wanted nothing more than to sit down and cry, but there was no time for that. Whatever the obstacles put in my way, I would grow taller to overcome them – failure was not an option! I wanted to ensure it would be easier for others – whether women or those who were perceived to come from a minority ethnic background – to follow in my footsteps.

PART 2

Approximately three years into my new role, I discovered I had a problem with my outer ear. Unable to get a doctor's appointment, I took myself to the Accident & Emergency department of my local hospital, and was told the trouble could be the result of stress. At the time, my health was generally good, though I did not exercise to any great degree (playing badminton on a Saturday morning was it!).

Deep down, I was aware that the Herculean task of holding a demanding full-time role and a scarcely less demanding part-time one was not sustainable. I resolved therefore to write to my bishop, who, after all, had pastoral responsibility for me. I hoped he would be in touch about possible part-time roles in the city.

There was no response to my letter. It seemed I would need to take matters into my own hands and search directly.

After not being shortlisted for two part-time roles in the City, I decided to ask the chair of the panel what essential criteria I was lacking. He phoned to say that he did not wish to put anything in writing, but would be happy to speak to me. Wanting an answer, I decided to meet him. He asked how many hours I worked in Parliament and I shared the number I was being paid for. It was clear that pursuing this avenue would not help his cause, so he then switched tack and told me they were looking for someone more Anglo-Catholic.

I felt he was making the assumption that because I was black I must be pentecostal or evangelical, so I responded robustly: 'If you knew anything of the church in Jamaica, you would be aware that it was staffed by the London Diocese with a United Society for the Propagation of the Gospel (USPG) influence.'

The truth is that walking around with any label sits uncomfortably with me. I am attracted to a role not because it's evangelical, liberal or Anglo-Catholic, but because, in my gut, it feels right. I will serve wherever I think I am being called to serve.

The chair of the panel then made the mistake of telling me that he did good research on those he shortlisted. I replied by reminding him that he'd previously shortlisted me for a role back in 2010. What he'd said when he entered the room where Ken and I were waiting was: 'I've come to get the next person for their interview, but I can see that they're not here.' Somehow, he did not connect the paperwork he was holding with the black face in front of him.

'Oh,' he said, 'I was hoping you would have forgotten that!'

'No, I haven't,' I replied.

'That will be one for your memoir,' he said.

'It will be one for yours too.' With that I bid him goodbye.

I'm not a person for conspiracy theories, but at one point I did wonder if there was a plot to punish me for taking the parliamentary role that others thought I should never have had. Had I been 'blacklisted'? Thankfully, my spirit was in a good place, so I did not dwell on thoughts of sinister manoeuvrings for long.

While I appreciated that the bishop I approached in another diocese made time to listen to my request, nothing came of it. He told me he had a full-time post that was about to be vacated and made into a part-time one. However, saying something is part-time does not necessarily decrease the expectations of parishioners, and this area was as challenging as the one I was about to leave. Even though I had a passion for working in such places, I had to think wisely. How could I give my best to both this role and the parliamentary one? In the end, I decided I would continue in Hackney until the right thing came along.

Then, at some point in a conversation with a friend, I heard she would be moving on from her role at a city church. Thinking this might be the fit I needed, I started to make enquiries. All in all, things progressed rather quickly and within months I was being licensed by the bishop to the post of Priest-in-charge at St Mary-at-Hill. The vicarage next door had been made into smaller flats and rented out, but fortunately alternative accommodation was found in Pimlico. By this stage, grandchildren were on the horizon, as Hannah and her husband David had a special guardianship order for baby Jayden. I was keen therefore to have a home where they and their children could come and visit with us.

One of the joys of St Mary-at-Hill was discovering that the founder of the Church Army had served there as Rector. One day, while standing at the altar, he had noticed there were more people walking past the door of the church than were inside, so he decided he would take church out onto the street. Being proficient on the trombone, he began playing to a gathered audience before sharing with them the good news of God's love. What an honour it was for me to be following in his footsteps now! His vision for the Church Army was that it would welcome both men and women to be evangelists, and I was standing in the place where the organisation had had its beginnings – and finding my joy for sharing the gospel undimmed.

Our farewell to Hackney finally took place in November 2014. The service was well attended, and my favourite caterer, Mr Hamilton of Plantation Inn, was employed to feed the 'five thousand' in Hackney Town Hall. People were gracious and generous, showering me with gifts and words of love, but in the depths of my being I was in mourning. Two weeks earlier, I had cried as I told my bishop I couldn't leave. I had loved this community unconditionally for sixteen years – the nice people as well as the prickly ones who sometimes make life challenging or uncomfortable. I can truly say that God filled me with grace to enable that love to be a reality. My parishioners clearly thought they were loved, because years later they are still in touch with me, keeping me informed of family situations like baptisms, weddings, serious illnesses or indeed funerals.

Moving from a six-bedroom Victorian vicarage to the smaller town house we'd kindly been offered turned out to be quite an emotional experience. I hadn't realised I was quite so attached to some of our furniture ... There was a beautiful dining room set, and family legend has it that I threatened not to cook Christmas dinner for everyone if I could not have this particular table (my wonderful and sensible husband had wanted something less ostentatious). Such was my strength of feeling that the room was large and needed something worthy of inhabiting the space, Ken felt he had no option but to give in. Now I was going to be parting with this lovely piece. Much as I would have loved to keep it, it was simply too big to fit into the dining room of the Pimlico house.

I hoped the table would go to a good home, like all the other items of furniture we proceeded to put in the front garden, such as lounge and bedroom suites (including a super-king-size bed) and an American fridge freezer. People literally came and helped themselves to what they required, and I'm glad I did not foolishly put things into storage, thinking I might make use of them in the future. Someone was making use of them now, and I felt assured that was a good thing. As the years go by, I am learning not to attach myself to 'stuff', but to hold lightly to things, so I can share what I have with others whose need might be greater.

We moved to Pimlico in February 2015 and soon settled in. Ken was superb, and never argued with me as I went about furnishing our new home. (He was, and continues to be, a real rock.) Moving to Pimlico meant far fewer hassles in terms of getting to Westminster each day. I no longer had heart-palpitating moments because of problems with the trains or worry that I would miss my connection.

I loved my time in Parliament and I'm proud of the many things I accomplished there. One was introducing prayers that spoke to situations we were living through at the time, such as severe civil unrest. For example, in 2012 a family-run furniture store in Croydon was set alight by rioters. Across some of our cities, cars too were set on fire and communities turned upside down. Instead of using the regular Psalm 67, which spoke of joy, I turned to Psalm 46: 'God is our refuge and strength, a very present help in trouble … The nations are in an uproar … "Be still, and know that I am God!"'

Indeed, when my time in Parliament came to an end, Jacob Rees-Mogg, the Leader of the House of Commons, commented on the way I led prayers in the House. Quoting from the regular Psalm 67 – 'Let the people praise thee, O God; let all the people praise thee. Then shall the earth yield her increase; and God, even our own God, shall bless us' (67:5-6, KJV) – he went on to say:

> These are beautiful, uplifting words that the Reverend Prebendary reads to us in her strong, resonant, resounding voice every morning when we meet in private to send up our petitions to God. It is when your chaplain, Mr Speaker, creates an atmosphere of prayer-fulness that it allows Right Hon. and Hon. Members to set their souls at ease with God as they prepare for the business ahead of them. She does so in a way that would move the heart of the most stony-hearted atheist to feel there is a true and a divine presence. To achieve this through the power of speech and the use of language is a great achievement, and one that has daily been the triumph of your chaplain, to the benefit of Members of Parliament.

Valerie Vaz, the Shadow Leader of the House, kindly paid tribute to my pastoral work:

> Reverend Rose has always been a visible presence and is often seen around Parliament, as she says, 'loitering with intent', comfortable in her own skin and 'in her hair'. I know that she has sought out Hon. Members when they have faced difficulties. We have not had to go to her;

194

she comes to us, and she makes sure that she counsels us in the appropriate way ... We certainly have felt the warmth of the Reverend Rose Hudson-Wilkin's spiritual leadership while she has been in Parliament and at a very exacting period of our history.

Patrick Grady, a member of the SNP, was similarly heartwarming:

Mr Speaker, one of your most significant legacies and early decisions is the appointment of Reverend Rose Hudson-Wilkin as your chaplain. I remember as a younger, keener but casual observer of business in this place reading some of the coverage and criticisms of that appointment at that time, but, as you have previously said, Mr Speaker, those critics were wrong in every single respect ... Prayers, especially in recent times, have provided some memorable moments, even if they have not always been visible to the public. Rose's choice of text often matches with uncanny ability the occasion of the day and hits the right note. At the start of our proceedings on the historic Saturday sitting a couple of weeks ago, she began with St Paul: 'Do not be anxious.' That was the moment that broke the ice, and chuckling could be heard across the chamber. By leading those prayers, Rose has ministered to the House collectively. Her presence in the Under Gallery, literally praying for us as we have taken part in some of the biggest and most historic votes of recent years, has not gone unnoticed. She has also ministered to many Members individually, as a chaplain, especially at times when tragedy has struck Parliament and the House.

Gavin Robinson from the DUP remarked:

The poetry she injected into Scripture brought it alive for us.

Sir David Lidington, speaking of the dreadful time in 2016 when Jo Cox MP was murdered in cold blood outside the library in which she was about to hold a constituency surgery, said:

… one of the things that is etched in my memory is how Members began to open up about threats that they had been suffering for quite some time. Whether it was about those things or a time of personal or family crisis or tragedy, Rose was always there: quiet, listening, offering comfort, and offering solidarity when it was most needed.[2]

PART 3

In the Chapel of St Mary Undercroft, in the Palace of Westminster, there is a door behind the organ. It leads to a broom cupboard in which one of the suffragettes, Emily Wilding Davison, hid on the night of the 1911 census. Women were not allowed the vote then. Ninety-nine years later, I was so glad to be able to serve in that place, officiating

---

2 Tributes to the Speaker's Chaplain on the occasion of her retirement from the House of Commons on 31st October 2019 (Hansard 31st October 2019)

at weddings and baptising Members' children and grand-children. I was always keen to make sure that I prepared those who came to the chapel for these offices well, even if it meant meeting with parents and godparents in their homes. These ceremonies were joyful occasions, and touchingly I still hear from several of those I met and ministered to.

When the UK's first female prime minister, Margaret Thatcher, died in 2013 and I learned that her body was to be brought into the Chapel of St Mary Undercroft, I decided to keep a vigil through the night and surround her with prayer. I understood the controversy surrounding Mrs Thatcher's political life and legacy, yet I'd been disturbed by the extremely negative reaction of some members of the public to her death. The next morning, when her coffin had been loaded into the hearse, I was driven by police vehicle to St Paul's Cathedral to take part in the service. There were many officers on the streets in expectation of disruption, but thankfully things stayed calm. The funeral was well attended, not only by present and past parliamentarians, but by national and international dignitaries too.

A year later, I held another vigil in the chapel, this time for Tony Benn, who had retired back in 2002 after forty-seven years as a Member of Parliament. I'd had the pleasure of getting to know him prior to his death, and the family asked me to conduct the internment, which would take place after the funeral service in St Margaret's Church, at a north London crematorium. I recall the journey to the crema-torium being a difficult one, as there were long hold-ups on the road. In the end we got out of the car and dived into the London Underground fully robed! The weird stares did not bother me, as the only thing on my mind was reaching the crematorium for the committal by the allocated time. Exiting the nearest tube station, our next challenge was to find a taxi, but for all these hiccups we arrived before many of the other mourners who'd set off in their cars (and quite possibly, if my memory serves me correctly, before the hearse).

The circumstances surrounding the vigil I kept in the chapel in 2017 were horrific. A terrorist, travelling by car at speed, began driving into pedestrians indiscriminately on Westminster Bridge. He then gained access to the parliamentary estate by foot, and proceeded to murder a policeman on duty, PC Keith Palmer, before being shot dead himself by armed officers. As the attack was unfolding, communication was limited and people were told to stay indoors in case a second terrorist had gained entry and was on the estate, waiting for an opportunity to strike. I felt a huge responsibility to be present and available to all those seeking reassurance and comfort. Many of PC Palmer's colleagues were understandably devastated and needed to talk, and it was a relief to me that the Metropolitan Police chaplain, Jonathan Osborne, was in attendance too. Jonathan and I had a good, mutually respectful working relationship, which made it possible to set about holding prayer vigil services. These enabled those affected to take a pause in the day and pay attention to what they were feeling, and some of the officers who have moved on to other duties or retired still talk about how much they appreciated our ministry. Jonathan and I took part in the funeral service, leading the procession from the parliamentary estate on foot, before joining the motorcade to Southwark Cathedral. In all, six people, including the terrorist, died as a result of the attack, and over fifty others were injured. It was a very dark time.

Over the years I served in Parliament, I met some deeply committed people who had chosen to enter politics with the sole purpose of making a difference in the communities they were elected to serve. The press and public alike love placing such folk on pedestals, and all too often, sadly, they are knocked off, with devastating consequences for their mental health and that of their families.

Others seemed to have few qualms about behaving badly. I watched with much sadness as Hon. Members defended or offered excuses for unacceptable behaviour ('the emperor has new clothes' is how I describe it). In my many engagements with the press as Chaplain to the Speaker, I made it clear that I would not be commenting on such stories. I felt I had a responsibility to MPs, as their pastor, to follow the example of the prophet Nathan and convey the truth privately, in whatever matter I could, to those who needed to hear it.

It seemed to me that the quality of our political discourse and life was being driven more by ideology than by a sense of justice and compassion. Take the whole Brexit debacle, with its slogan 'Take back control'. What have we taken back control of? What I see is (a) that our children and grandchildren have lost the freedom of movement we once had; (b) an ugly nationalism that has forgotten what it means to be human, and (c) a fractured political system desperately trying to sustain itself by creating division within the community. I have lived in Britain since 1985, but it was during Brexit that I was shouted at and told to go back to Africa!

Brexit created a toxic environment, one which I firmly believed contributed to the murder of Jo Cox MP (mentioned earlier) by an individual who can only be described as a far-right extremist. I am yet to be convinced that Parliament has truly reflected on the consequences of the ideological game we embarked on as a country. I believe we need a new kind of political engagement, in which we do not collude with injustice because we want our party to win at all costs, but think about issues of wider responsibility beyond the few. We need a more compassionate politics instead of the confrontational, self-interested one we have, which plays one group off against another.

Prime Minister's Questions (PMQs) on Wednesdays at noon could be particularly embarrassing to watch. Parliamentarians – supposedly grown adults responsible for making the laws of our country – would heckle one another, as if they still belonged to a particularly rowdy university debating society. I did speak to Members about this and was told that it was 'theatre'. (When my daughter Amanda once attended PMQs, she left before the end because she found it so excruciatingly embarrassing, witnessing such bad behaviour from people meant to be leaders.) I was sometimes told, 'Rose, you know that later we'll all go for a drink together!'

'Yes,' I said, 'but those watching don't know that. They just see you tearing one another apart.'

I hope that I spoke truth to power during my time in Parliament. I am often asked if I miss being there, and my reply is always this: 'While I was there, I enjoyed it and I still pray for parliamentarians. I do recognise within me, however, the feeling that if John Bercow were still in office, I would have been very sad to leave him behind. It is good that we departed at the same time.'

I had and still have a lot of time and admiration for John. I found in him someone who genuinely cared about those in society who are treated as underdogs, and he used his office to make a difference. There were many things he set out to achieve on which he was strongly opposed, such as the introduction of an Education Centre. Today thousands of children from across the country come through that centre. John made it possible for there to be a nursery on the parliamentary estate, though he faced much resistance to this too, perhaps because the nursery would be using the space that once hosted a pub. He held to his conviction and today that nursery is a valuable resource for parents and carers. When others said no to my appointment as the next Chaplain to the Speaker, John gave an unqualified and unconditional yes. He withstood opposition and in doing so created history. He also introduced the Youth Parliament, in which young people (who some objected would leave chewing-gum on the historic green seats in the Commons chamber) engage in debate. I believe it should be compulsory to watch them if you wish to be a professional politician! They listen respectfully to one another and present their arguments with confidence. It is my hope that some of these young people will become involved in helping us change the way we engage with one another politically. Finally, as Speaker, John enabled backbenchers to have much more input into the political agenda.

I was saddened to learn of the accusations brought against John that made him persona non grata. **I never personally witnessed him bullying anyone**, but this does not negate others' accounts of their experience. For the record, I want to say that if I had ever witnessed bullying behaviour, I would have addressed this with him. I believe history will be kinder to Speaker John Bercow and the changes he achieved than may seem likely now.

On many occasions I've been heard to remark that my years in Hackney were the best years of my life. I've meant every word, but as I reflect on my ministry as Chaplain to the Speaker, I feel lucky to be able to say that those years were equally enjoyable. I loved the interactions I had with the security team, the cooks, cleaners, staff and parliamentarians of both Houses. I took part in many historic occasions, such as the procession for the State Opening of Parliament. And, of course, I met many international leaders such as the Dalai Lama, Aung San Suu Kyi, the former President of Myanmar, Justin Trudeau, the Premier of Canada, and the President of the United Sates of America …

I'd been asked to wait in Central Lobby. Speaker Bercow and President Barack Obama came out of the House of Lords. They walked towards me and stopped on their way into the Commons chamber. There I was introduced as the seventy-ninth parliamentary chaplain. The President was even more handsome in real life! With a rather youthful look, he smiled and said to me, 'Man, you look spiff.' The coat dress I was wearing that day has ever since been known as my Barack Obama outfit. In reply, I told him this was my 'Nunc dimittis' moment. It really was!

Something else I will always treasure was playing a part in organising and delivering a memorial event to celebrate the life of my great hero, President Nelson Mandela. Westminster Hall was filled, and we'd made sure to invite many young people from neighbouring secondary schools. We also secured a London-based South African choir, which gave a wonderful rendition of the South African national anthem. As part of my contribution, I read from the poem 'Invictus' by William Ernest Henley, while the Speakers of both Houses led the tributes.

That same day, I'd been due to record *Desert Island Discs* on Radio 4. It nearly didn't happen! I felt I needed to concentrate on getting ready for the memorial, but Ken pointed out that the programme was a significant one, and encouraged me to find a way to fit it in. The BBC kindly provided a taxi after the recording, but I literally had to exit along Whitehall and run towards Parliament wearing my crimson robe. Quite a spectacle to behold!

I don't think I fully realised how wide an audience *Desert Island Discs* attracted, and perhaps that was just as well. It was so difficult choosing just eight songs. Having got my list down to eleven, I hoped when I shared the significance of each, I would be allowed to include them all, but the researcher I met made it quite clear that wouldn't be possible. In the end, as discussed with my host Kirsty Young, I settled for these ...

My first choice was Arrow's 'Hot Hot Hot', a calypso song that makes me dance with wanton abandonment wherever I happen to be, not caring who may be watching!

My second was George Frideric Handel's 'Zadok the Priest', performed by the Choir of Westminster Abbey, to reflect my royal connections and deep admiration for the Queen – a young woman who was set apart at an early age and anointed for her role.

My third was Jimmy Cliff's 'Many Rivers to Cross'. I had attended several funerals in my patch due to black-on-black killings and there is something haunting about the lyrics of that song. To me it speaks of one's life spiralling out of control, and this is so real for the young people caught up in these acts of self-destruction. I feel the pain conveyed in the song, and I connect it with the pain I have seen etched on the faces of families in mourning for their loved ones.

My fourth choice was 'Respect', recorded by Aretha Franklin. In my mind, I place this song against the backdrop of the atrocities committed in South Africa and other parts of the world. And it buoys me up whenever I'm treated with disrespect, which continues to this day.

Barry White's 'You're My First, My Last, My Everything' was my fifth choice, because Ken sang it to me on the occasion of our twenty-fifth wedding anniversary celebrations. I told the full story back in Chapter 7!

The spiritual 'There is a Balm in Gilead', sung by the Adventist Vocal Ensemble, was my sixth song choice. The group performs with great passion and meaning, and the song speaks to me of the healing balm to be found in the presence of God. It often soothes my soul on weary days, and I would like to think that I encourage this kind of healing balm in the communities I serve. Ken Burton, the Ensemble's director and arranger, has brought the group to perform at many memorable events for me, including my consecration.

My seventh choice was the iconic 'Something Inside so Strong', mentioned earlier, by Labi Siffre. It is a song that speaks of the barriers others can put in our way, and the option we have of simply growing taller to overcome such obstacles.

My eighth and final song choice was Harry Belafonte's 'Island in the Sun', which is a strong reminder of my roots and where I come from. I may have British citizenship, but my Jamaican heritage runs through my veins and has contributed enormously to who I am today.

The book I chose was the complete works of Maya Angelou (another of my heroes) and my luxury to take was lots of earrings!

Truly, between recording *Desert Island Discs* and taking part in Nelson Madela's memorial tribute, 12 December 2013 was a day that has never stopped giving. Simply full of amazing once-in-a-lifetime memories!

17
A CALL TO BE BISHOP OF DOVER

RELAXING ON HOLIDAY IN MALAGA with Hannah and the grandchildren, I happened to look at my phone and see that the Archbishops' Appointments Secretary had been trying to reach me. Immediately, I was plunged into turmoil.

I bet I'm being contacted because my name's been put forward again, I thought. My dilemma was that I had recently decided I would no longer allow myself to be considered for senior roles, previous applications having been unsuccessful, and had written to both archbishops to express this clearly. I've always believed that it's the people of a diocese who should call you to serve them, and that no one is entitled or has a right to be a bishop, and I still hold to that.

To be frank, this 'confidential' pathway to senior leadership roles in the Church is no walk in the park! If your name is offered for consideration, and after prayerful thought you feel it is right to let it go forward, you will be asked to produce substantial pieces of work by specific deadlines, all the while continuing seamlessly with your usual schedule, as you simply can't reveal to your colleagues or congregation that there is another heavy demand on your time. Significantly, you also have to start imagining yourself in the role you're applying for, because it's only by inhabiting it that you'll get into the frame of mind necessary to prepare yourself well.

Not long before this, I had accepted my name being in the mix for a post I felt was a good fit, and was told that not being shortlisted to it had to do with leadership: apparently, I 'did not have the leadership ability to fulfil it'. I was deeply hurt; more than that, I felt scarred by this thoughtless comment and believed I could no longer offer myself to a church that was determined by its actions to tell me I was not good enough. The fact was that I'd been engaged in church leadership from a very young age and had actually served longer in ministry than many others who had been promoted to senior roles.

Ken, noticing my carefree holiday mood had changed, listened carefully as I expressed my troubled thoughts. After staying silent for a while, he urged me not to close the door but to let my name go through; he had great confidence in me. He felt so strongly about this that I eventually gave up resisting and relented. But the struggle and confusion I was experiencing inside remained intense.

Having a supportive spiritual director, I sought her wisdom and her prayers. In our session together, I was left with an image of going through a pregnancy that had resulted in no baby at the end. The pregnancy was inhabiting and envisioning myself in the various roles I was applying for. When each failed to come to fruition, I was left with a real sense of loss.

Following one rejection, a discerning young man in the local community named Nathaniel, who had been aware that the search for a new bishop was underway, had shared his excitement that he hoped it would be me. Without going into any detail, I felt I had to tell him that this was not going to be the case. He paused and looked at me directly. 'Sister

Rose,' he said, 'you do not need a title to be our bishop. You are already our bishop.'

I just about held back the tears. His comment touched me deeply, and those words will be forever etched in my memory. It was clear that I did not need the institution of the Church to confer a title on me. To the people I was serving, I was their chief pastor!

On our return from Spain, the wheels spun into motion as I addressed the list of practical and preparatory tasks to be completed. My small prayer cell, without knowing the detail, was already at the work of prayer, and when the day of the interview came, I felt as if I had nothing to lose. I went in saying to God that it was all in his hands, but I couldn't help adding that this would be the last time!

When the interview came to an end, I was asked if I had any questions and I replied that I didn't. However, as the members of the panel began to rise from their seats, I heard myself blurt out, 'Actually, I do have something to say, but it's not really a question.'

They settled back down expectantly.

'You know when some people are missing a few essential criteria and you say, "Not to worry; we can put things in place to assist them," and then when others are missing just a couple of the essential criteria you say no? Well, I just want you to know that I am capable of being trained.'

With that I thanked them for listening before exiting the room. Others were being interviewed, so I would not hear further until the following day.

The next day arrived. Early afternoon came and went. Once more I assumed that it was not to be, and felt at peace.

After all, I had carefully prepared myself for a no. I set off for evensong at St Paul's Cathedral, but along the way found myself distracted as I began to attempt to formulate the words I would say to the archbishops about *definitely* not wanting my name to be put forward again.

The good thing about attending evensong in a cathedral is that worries tend to fade. Instead, you find yourself bathed in the music and the angelic sound of the choir, or lost in the architectural beauty of the building. St Paul's was a good place to be as I pondered how to take yet another rejection – a true 'balm in Gilead'. As evensong progressed, I experienced a real calm. I felt ready for a no, and knew instinctively that all would be well, whatever the response turned out to be.

At the end of the service, I joined the procession out to the Dean's Aisle – past the statue of poet and former Dean John Donne, who spoke so eloquently of humanity's inter-dependence and of 'being involved in mankind'. It was while removing my robes that I looked at my phone and saw that the Archbishop of Canterbury had tried to contact me earlier in the day. I was sure that the answer was going to be no, but felt I had to call back.

The reception was patchy and made for a difficult listen. 'Let me go outside,' I said. 'I may be able to hear you better there.'

As I made my way to the nearest exit, I suddenly realised that the Archbishop was telling me the panel had said yes. This could not be real! I had been accepted for the suffragan see of Dover! The tears began to flow. I simply wept.

Ken and I had arranged to meet that evening to attend a private screening of a German film called *Where Hands*

Touch. When he saw my eyes were red from crying, he assumed the worst and attempted to console me.

'It was a yes!' I blurted out.

I found myself enveloped in a huge hug. 'Really!' he said.

We could not tell our friends or family. We had to wait for the Prime Minister's office and the Queen to agree a date for the announcement. There was a thrill in waiting for all to be revealed. Yet it was also beginning to dawn on me that I would not only be leaving Parliament, I'd be moving home to a part of the country I scarcely knew.

My consecration would take place at St Paul's on 19 November 2019. The cathedral team welcomed my involvement in the planning. I invited the former Archbishop of York, John Sentamu, to preach and John Bercow to read one of the lessons. The Archbishop of the Province of the West Indies, Howard Gregory, and the Archbishop of Southern Africa, Thabo Makgoba, would be joining the Bishop of London, Sarah Mullally, in presenting me. It then transpired that the nominated Bishop of Reading, Archdeacon Olivia Graham, would be consecrated at the same time, and needed to contribute to the content of the service too. I felt I could not withdraw my invitation to either John, but my daughter Amanda was happy to stand down from her reading and to read instead at my installation at Canterbury Cathedral (which would follow two weeks later).

Regarding the music for the service, I asked the London Adventist Chorale to take part, and also a young man named Jermain Jackman, who won the BBC's singing competition *The Voice* in 2014. Jermain was four years old when I arrived at my church in Hackney. Once his gifting was known, I got him singing at a variety of Sunday services. Hearing him at our Christmas midnight service was always a thrilling experience and having him sing at my consecration would be very special indeed. Archdeacon Olivia was extremely understanding and happily gave her input to the general music on the day.

The Revd Canon Calvin McIntyre and his wife Camille decided from the moment they heard of my appointment that they were coming. It was a delight too that the Holloways – George and Lynn – were going to attend. Like the McIntyres, they were long-time friends. Two other priests from Jamaica, Canons Perrin and Kitson, who recognised the historical significance of my appointment, also booked their flight, as did Nicholas Dill, the Bishop of Bermuda (who had previously invited me to lead a retreat for the clergy of Bermuda). I felt sad that my adopted mom, Faye Jolly, was unwell and would not be able to travel and, of course, my precious daddy, Horace Whittingham, had already gone to be with the Lord. However, I was most encouraged that one of his sons, Wayne, would be present, along with his wife Pam.

My dear sister Shirley was so excited for me. Although she hated long flights, this was one she was not going to miss! Her husband Peat and their youngest daughter, Jhulia, would be flying with her. Although my mother did not tell me directly, she disclosed to Shirley that she wanted to attend. I hoped that being present for such an occasion would be special for her. After all, this was the little girl she had sent away. Whatever her reason at the time, like Joseph sold by his brothers into slavery, God had meant it for good (Genesis 50:20)! Numerous friends from my high school days also made the trip, and there were representatives from the Episcopal Church too.

On the day of the consecration, St Paul's Cathedral was pretty near full, with many of my friends from the UK joining those from all over the globe. The evening before, Archbishop Justin and Caroline Welby had hosted a relaxing supper for Olivia and me and our close families, who were staying at Lambeth, and they joined us too for breakfast on the day itself. My guests and I then set off in the transport that had been arranged. There were a number of vehicles involved, and when I got to the cathedral, I was rather perturbed to find some family members were yet to arrive; notably, we were missing the taxi bearing my mother and Shirley.

As I had to do my legal swearing and signing of the declaration and oaths before the start of the ceremony, it soon got to the point when I could no longer wait outside. The cathedral was filling up with literally hundreds and hundreds of people; there was a real buzz in the air! However, my distraction meant I failed to notice that my stipendiary role as Chaplain to the Speaker was not recorded (as would have been correct) on the legal papers, but rather my voluntary one of Priest Vicar of Westminster Abbey.

In any case, I was soon completely caught up in the service. Around the time of my anointing, as I'd requested, Jermain Jackman sang 'Precious Lord, Take My Hand'. This iconic gospel song was performed by the great Mahalia Jackson at the funeral of Martin Luther King Jr. Having the words sung at the end of the life of such a towering figure and at the beginning of my consecration journey – in this instance by an exceptional young man I had been proud to nurture – was profoundly moving. As I knelt before the Archbishop, surrounded by many other bishops laying hands on me, the tears flowed freely. John Sentamu reached over to pass me a pack of tissues! This was most welcome as I had none in my pocket, not having anticipated the need.

At the end of the service, I felt carried from the cathedral on the crest of a wave, so heartfelt were the cheers that greeted Olivia and me as we processed down the aisle with the Archbishop in the middle. For the first time, I was carrying my wooden crozier, made from Blue Mahoe, the national tree of Jamaica, and gifted to me by my Jamaican friends in attendance. I tried to spot who was in the congregation, but it was not easy to pick out faces. I did see the footballer John Barnes, and learned later that the eminent newsreader Sir Trevor McDonald OBE had also attended (my friend Alexandra sent me the selfie she'd taken with him!), along with many of the parliamentarians I'd ministered to.

It was a thrill to be greeted by the crowds on the steps of the cathedral and there were many photo requests. By the time I got away, the buses back to Lambeth where the reception was being held had already left. Anna Drew, the diocesan Director of Communications, took the initiative and called a taxi to take us to Lambeth Palace for the reception.

The Welbys had kindly offered me the use of one of their rooms, and I'd again invited my favourite caterer, the Hamiltons of Plantation Inn, to prepare Jamaican cuisine for us all. When we arrived, many people had already taken their seats, while some of my family guests were being directed upstairs to the reception hosted by the Welbys for the visiting bishops. I should have made an appearance there too, but got completely caught up in greeting so many friends I was seeing for the first time in ages. In the meanwhile, a few of the bishops came downstairs briefly to join my reception. There was so much joy and goodwill! Something special had happened that day; perhaps in years to come, the significance of it would become clearer.

When the celebrations came to an end, Ken and I, along with twelve other family members and friends who would be staying with me in Canterbury, drove to west London to the Jamaican High Commission. There, the Jamaican High Commissioner to London, His Excellency Seth George Ramocan, presented me with the Order of Distinction (Commander Class) that had been awarded to me by the Jamaican government earlier in the year. Among the guests in attendance were staff and well-wishers from the diaspora, who joined us for refreshments after the formal ceremony. Late that evening, Ken and my guests and I left for my new county, Kent ('The Garden of England'), and our new home, 52 St Martins Hill, Canterbury, in what might best be described as a state of weary elation! We had witnessed and experienced history in the making: the first woman of colour becoming a bishop in the Church of England!

The following two weeks passed quickly. My brother-in-law assumed the role of chef, ably assisted by my friends. We were still riding on the crest of a wave, and it was so good to have my sister Shirley with me, but there was not much opportunity to reminisce. In a heartbeat, it seemed, it was Saturday 30 November, and time for my installation at Canterbury Cathedral. I was most looking forward to the anthem, and the choir did a magnificent job, as reported in the press back home:

'Jah is My Keeper', a composition by Jamaican reggae icon Peter Tosh, sounded mystically within the ancient walls of the celebrated Canterbury Cathedral in England yesterday afternoon, during the service of installation for Jamaica-born Rose Hudson-Wilkin, the new Bishop of Dover.

'Jah is indeed my keeper, and those words will sustain me', the newly enthroned bishop told *The Sunday Gleaner* after the service.

'And I think Peter Tosh would be surprised with great joy if he were alive to hear the choir of Canterbury Cathedral performing his composition so beautifully', she added.

My only regret is that the anthem was not recorded. However, Peter's daughter had news of the performance and wrote me a lovely letter of congratulations. The cathedral was packed, with a good number of the overseas friends who had attended my consecration again on hand, and many of my previous parishioners from Hackney. All their joys were my joy too! That evening is indelibly imprinted on my mind, due to the extraordinary outpouring of support and encouragement I witnessed and experienced first-hand. Among my well-wishers were some great prayer warriors, and I was to discover that there were formidable prayer warriors in my new dioceses too. I felt I was in good hands.

Later that evening in the chapter house, where we gathered for refreshments, those from the Episcopal Church gifted me a white mitre (the hat worn by a bishop) that had the African Kente cloth as its main feature.

One of the cathedral's former organists wrote a musical anthem based on a passage of Scripture from Habakkuk I had learned from my adopted mom: 'Though the fig tree is not budding and the vine beareth no fruit ... yet will I rejoice in the Lord.' These are words she describes as getting her through many tough times. Why would I choose such a passage for a celebratory service? Simply because I recognised, as probably no one else could, how shaped I had been by my life's journey up to that date. The road I had travelled had been one of rejection, abuse and conflict; yet it had also been one of resilience, exploration and joy. Through everything, I had been consciously aware of the presence of God watching over me, carrying me and strengthening me to the core.

So the passage not only reminded me of everything I have to keep me rejoicing; it meant dear Faye was there with me in spirit too!

18
REVELATION

MY FIRST TASK ON THE SUNDAY immediately following my installation was to ordain a priest (he was already a deacon but had not been ordained to the priesthood along with his cohort). I carefully planned my sermon and familiarised myself with the structure of the service. However, I discovered I was less prepared in other ways ... For example, I found I kept looking at my hands, not only when I was at prayer, but at odd moments, as I was washing, driving or doing the shopping. These hands of mine were about to become the conduit of something very special.

Officiating at this my first ordination service impacted me in a big way. Physically I was in the moment while acutely aware that something else was at work. I felt a deep connection with what had happened to me only two weeks earlier and was about to happen again. Though very nervous, I knew this was a moment when the Spirit of the living God would be falling afresh on us; it was a 'Mary moment' when a 'yes' would make possible all that was yet to come; a 'God moment'. It was not about Rose at all.

There were other times in those early days when, looking back now, I realise I was grappling with imposter syndrome: sometimes, I asked myself if I was really sure I was in the right place! On one occasion, at the opening of a new school,

223

I spoke at the pupils' assembly and enjoyed refreshments with the governing body before the formal part of the morning began. A few words were exchanged, and I was invited to unveil the commemorative plaque. It read something like 'Benenden Church of England Primary School was opened by The Right Revd Rose Hudson-Wilkin, Bishop of Dover, on 06.12.19'. Pulling the cord to draw back the curtain, I found myself having what I can only describe as an out-of-body experience, as I heard my voice saying out loud, 'That's my name!'

I've been approached by people after various services with responses that have rendered me speechless. A man in his early nineties told me I had woken him up; another in his seventies confided after a confirmation service, 'I have never believed in the ordination of women or in women bishops, but you have just changed my mind.' (This is said quite often, but never ceases to amaze me!)

I must be frank and share that a handful of people have told me they do not accept my ministry, because I am a woman. These souls all appear to have a hotline to God, who has (apparently) made it clear that men are in the entitled position of being God's gift, and are therefore equipped to speak to everyone, male and female, young and old, irrespective of colour, creed or culture. Women, on the other hand, by virtue of their gender, are not suited to addressing audiences that include men, but only those of women and children.

I am supposed to accept that this is the same God who called on Mary to carry and bear the living Word; the same God who made it possible for the women at the tomb to be the first apostles and charged them to tell the disciples that

Christ was risen. I am supposed to accept that the Christ who said, 'The harvest is plentiful, but the labourers are few; therefore ask the Lord of the harvest to send out labourers into his harvest' (Matthew 9:37–38), meant female labourers to be excluded simply because they were women!

I always listen politely to those who tell me they do not wish to receive my ministry before letting them know that I do not really care if they accept my ministry or not. My interest is in the gospel. Whenever they're ready to live out the gospel, I'll be ready to join them in that mission.

From an early age, whenever I thought of God and faith, I would connect this with the idea of discovering and becoming my best self. It never occurred to me that being a woman placed a limit on me; my experience has always been of a generous God – and that suggests the complete opposite.

I was under no illusion about my entry into the world. I do not believe I was a longed-for child: my parents appear to have conceived me accidentally, whether in the course of a single or a multiplicity of sexual encounters, and nothing in my early experience fills me with any confidence that they had a plan. Nor do I get a sense that the harsh living conditions both knew, and the brutality with which they were treated, allowed them the space to dream of a better life for their children.

Being so young when Aunt Pet told Shirley and me that our mother and father did not care enough for us immediately created a yearning and a longing for more. My adopted mom and dad, in living out their faith, showed me something beautiful: a God who would love me unconditionally and without prejudice; a God who knew me before I was born. In the words of the psalmist: 'For it was you who formed my inward parts; you knit me together in my mother's womb. I praise you, for I am fearfully and wonderfully made. Wonderful are your works; that I know very well' (Psalm 139:13–14).

I wanted to live a life of faithfulness to God.

Shirley and I may have been physically apart, but we have always maintained an unbroken bond and found ways of staying in touch with each other. She too had passed her eleven-plus exam – she was so much brighter than me academically! – and had chosen to attend the Convent of Mercy Academy 'Alpha', an educational institution sponsored by the Sisters of Mercy in the Roman Catholic Archdiocese of Jamaica. An arrangement was made with the staff for her to board there and return home at weekends. This was a real blessing, as it allowed Shirley space to breathe. Keen to become the best she could be (as I was seeking to do), she set her heart on a nursing career, and after doing well in her O-level exams eventually qualified as a midwife. Sometime later, Kaiser Permanente, one of America's leading healthcare providers, headhunted her! By then, Shirley had married her childhood sweetheart, Peat, and they went on to have three children and three grandchildren.

It meant the world to me to have my big sister present at the beginning of my ministry as a bishop. She, more than anyone, knows the journey I have been on to get to this point. My story is her story, and her story is mine. Today, Shirley is retired from nursing and is a pastor in the Church of God in California. Like me, she has experienced the generosity of our great God, and will never let go. I do sometimes wish that we were geographically closer, but WhatsApp takes care of that, and I am content to have her in my corner, a great prayer warrior. She looks after our mother, who lives with her most of the year.

Shirley is a great example of what it means to live forgiveness. She would be the first to say that she is a work in progress. I am extremely proud of her.

One of my priorities as a bishop has been to visit schools, both primary and secondary. I enjoy doing Q&As with the young people, and something I regularly get asked is, 'What does a bishop do?'

'Great question!' I'll reply, before going on to explain that my role is a bit like that of their head teacher. I have overall responsibility for a geographical area (albeit a much wider one), and pastoral responsibility for all the ministers who serve within it. As a bishop, I ordain, license and commission those starting out in ministry. For example, at the licensing of a new priest to their parish, I hand them their licence and say the following words, 'Receive this Cure of Souls, which is both mine and yours …' I also confirm all those who wish to affirm their faith. And I preach and celebrate at the Eucharist.

In sharing these details with school students, I'm keen to let them know that I'm interested not only in the people who come to church and practise their faith, but in the people who never come to church and would profess to have no faith at all. This means that, as a bishop, I'm always ready to speak prophetically in the public square regarding the God of love who cares about the needs of those who are hungry, thirsty, sick and in prison and who need to be clothed (see Matthew 25:35–40).

My passion is to be on the edge with the lost, the last and the least.

Being called on to speak at numerous engagements, in a variety of contexts and on a range of themes, is something a bishop learns to expect. I have not often been puzzled as to what to say, but one invitation from the Women's Institute (WI) did leave me lost for words. My briefing paper specified they had asked for my contribution not to have any religious content. I was flabbergasted! I am a bishop. Why would you ask a bishop to address your organisation if you did not want them to say anything about faith? I was keen to visit the WI nevertheless, because the branch was within the diocese and I like to respond to as many local requests as possible.

On the day, I was met by one of the organisers and again reminded that the content of my address should not be religious. I entered the room resolving simply to relate the story of my journey to becoming Bishop of Dover. Speaking of my childhood experiences, however, at one point I felt myself pause … The next moment, my voice was saying that I was presently writing my autobiography, and what I was about to disclose, I had not planned to include in the book.

And then I told them this.

'I was raped and sexually abused from a young age. Two of my older cousins' boyfriends were involved, but it did not stop there: there was also abuse associated with the Church by so-called religious men. I have never spoken about this before, probably due to a determination not to be defined by what happened to me. I was not going to become anyone's victim. In the words of Bob Marley's "Buffalo Soldier", my childhood was one of "fighting for survival". As such, it is part of a much larger story that tells of a world in which men exercise their dominance by subjugating those deemed to be the weaker sex. My experience was not unusual – this is not just about me! Many girls and young women of my acquaintance were similarly exploited. The reality was that even on public transport, in broad daylight, one did not feel safe.'

When I stopped for breath, the response in the room was overwhelming. Deeply empathetic, the WI members wanted to know how I could have got through such challenges. How was I still standing? I had to tell them that, frankly, without my faith I would not be who I am and where I am today.

These dear women who'd wanted to hear nothing of religion urged me that my story, which speaks of courage and survival, must be widely shared.

The role of a suffragan bishop is to assist their diocesan bishop. However, for many years now, the suffragan Bishop of Dover has exercised a diocesan role in the Diocese of Canterbury, and this involves attending the General Synod of the Church of England. There are many things I enjoy doing as Bishop of Dover. This task, however (I am well aware), I do out of duty.

I find it painful to listen to many of the contributions, especially when I detect at heart a misogyny often covered in religiosity ('The Bible says'), or when I hear people who expect the status quo to remain untouched happily invoking the name of God in a way that almost seeks to shut down discussion.

I have had to pay attention as people have made proud speeches about keeping their virginity (saving themselves), when all I wanted to do was scream, 'Some of us had no choice! It was taken from us!' I never walk away from the debating chamber, as I am there on behalf of the diocese, but I am greatly pained by the many entitled men and women jumping up and down and shrieking loudly about matters to do with sex!

I believe very strongly that the Church bears some responsibility for the abuse that women and girls suffer in our society and in our world today. While we continue to teach and practise a male superiority, we cannot address such issues with any integrity. We must stop institutionalising such a differentiation between men and women, and instead promote a respectful partnership in the circle of life.

When I spend time in schools, and the children ask me what I enjoy the most, I am eager to share that being with them is life-giving. They are trusting, not afraid to tell you what is on their mind, free and open. How God must long for us, his Church, to be as trusting, honest and open to the Spirit flowing among us! Instead, we are defensive and behave as if God is asking us to protect him. If God needs me to protect him, then I need a bigger God.

Today, as I reflect on my journey so far, I feel deeply thankful. I am grateful that my daughters are confident young women who know they are made in the image of God. They understand well that letting their light shine will enable others to let their light shine too and thus become all God wants them to be. In the words of John 10:10, 'I came that they may have life, and have it abundantly.'

I am grateful that my children have had a great father, and that I have an amazing husband who is assured in himself, with nothing to prove and able to stand shoulder to shoulder with his wife. This brings me joy. Throughout our journey together he has loved me unconditionally, often telling me 'You can' when he sees me thinking that I can't. In a recent birthday card, he wrote: '62, and still as beautiful as ever. You are happy in work, blessed by your children and grand-children. Adored by your husband and welcomed by all who meet you. May your years be many and your love be strong …'

Wow, that he thinks this after forty years of marriage! What more could I ask for?

Finally, this girl from Montego Bay is eternally thankful for the hand of God that has strengthened me each step of the way. The sad experiences I've endured have made me stronger; they have filled me with compassion for those from the underside, those on the edge, the women and girls who continue to be abused in the Church and around the world.

Forty-nine years after hearing God's call to serve, I am still full of passion for the gospel. Living the gospel is where my focus lies. It is indeed my heartbeat.

Here I am, Lord. Send me!